Preaching and Politics

Preaching and Politics

Engagement without Compromise

TIM J. R. TRUMPER

WIPF & STOCK · Eugene, Oregon

PREACHING AND POLITICS
Engagement without Compromise

Copyright © 2009, Tim J. R. Trumper. All rights reserved. Except for brief quotations in critical publications or reviews, no part of this book may be reproduced in any manner without prior written permission from the publisher. Write: Permissions, Wipf and Stock Publishers, 199 W. 8th Ave., Suite 3, Eugene, OR 97401.

Wipf & Stock
A Division of Wipf and Stock Publishers
199 W. 8th Ave., Suite 3
Eugene, OR 97401
www.wipfandstock.com

ISBN 13: 978-1-60608-008-5

Manufactured in the U.S.A.

All Bible quotations are from the New King James Version (Nashville, Thomas Nelson, 1983) or the English Standard Version (Wheaton, Illinois, Crossway Bibles, 2002), unless otherwise stated.

*For the glory of Christ—
the divine agent of eternal change*

Our Father, remove from us the sophistication of our age and the skepticism that has come, like frost, to blight our faith and to make it weak. Bring us back to a faith that makes men great and strong, a faith that enables us to love and to live, the faith by which we are triumphant, the faith by which alone we can walk with Thee.

We pray for a return of that simple faith, that old-fashioned trust in God, that made strong and great the homes of our ancestors who built this good land and who in building left us our heritage. In the strong name of Jesus, our Lord, we make this prayer. Amen.

—THE PRAYERS OF PETER MARSHALL

Contents

Preface ix

1 A Middle Way 1

  The Method of the Biblical-Political Approach

2 A Spiritual Way 17

  The Propriety of the Biblical-Political Approach

3 A Practical Way 54

  The Application of the Biblical-Political Approach

Conclusion 81

Appendix A 87
Appendix B 89
Appendix C 91
Bibliography 93

Preface

The effort to think like a Christian about politics is a worthy task for believers in all times and places, but it is an especially important task today.... Elsewhere around the world Christian concerns are now more visible than anyone could ever have thought possible even a decade ago.

—Mark A. Noll,
Adding Cross to Crown[1]

The British Prime Minister Harold Wilson once famously observed that, "a week is a long time in politics." Whether he was quoting Benjamin Franklin or not, he was right; all the more so given today's saturation coverage of politics. And not only so far as the politicians are concerned, but for all those who keep track of its ebb and flow.

For admittedly selfish reasons, I have frequently hoped over recent months for a way to pause politics, if only to ensure the application and illustration of my argument does not become dated before it appears in print. I rest in the thought that although set in a time, space, and history context, the present study deals with principles of abiding relevance for pulpit ministry. I also hold out the hope that while, over time, my asides will inevitably appear dated, they may still provide an interesting glimpse into the socioreligious aspect of the Anglo-American context at the end of the opening decade of the third millennium.

1. Noll, *Adding Cross to Crown*, 15.

For the record, *Preaching and Politics* was written in skeletal form prior to the 2006 U.S. elections, but "enfleshed," lengthened, and edited more recently during the 2008 Presidential election.[2] The study reflects the lessons of those elections—lessons which continue to be before us to one degree or another as we begin a new four-year cycle of politics. The change of incumbent party and the inauguration of a new President do nothing to diminish the burden of my argument. In fact, if the fears of many are at all warranted, the principles addressed hereafter are more relevant than ever. For it is in the realm of politics that we have a most significant battlefield of the unfolding culture war, the unending (re-)configurations of which will go on unrelentingly until Christ comes again.[3] The stability of inscripturated revelation makes

2. *Preaching and Politics* was originally titled *Politics and the Pulpit*. The change of title came about to reflect the book's prioritization of the theme of pulpit ministry.

3. While very enthused about Cal Thomas's and Bob Beckel's *Common Ground*, I beg to differ from their assessment that "the so-called culture war is really a small battle, being fought between polarizers on the right and left, while the vast majority of Americans refuse to be involved." I do so, first, because "a small battle" tells us nothing in itself of the size of the issues we face today. History is peppered with examples of small battles that have been waged with hindsight over humongous issues, simply because societies have failed to see or to feel the importance of the principles at stake. Secondly, even supposing the culture war is "a small battle" it can nevertheless be fought over critical issues of relevance to the majority, especially when those issues have to do with our basic outlook on life (worldview). Thirdly, I differ on the basis of the fact that the culture war is not "a small battle" but an endless series of conflicts. Together these amount to a war that is real and not "so-called." Fourthly, I deny that passion about the culture war makes one of necessity a polarizer. There are many of us outside the realm of politics who are in this culture war for neither money nor fame, but for truth. We fight not because we are war profiteers, but because God's will is being flouted and humankind is suffering accordingly. Fifthly, I question whether the vast majority have in fact refused to be involved. Quite the contrary, it is becoming increasingly difficult to evade the culture war. At the ballot

it possible, however, to lay out in the midst of the forest a sure path by which we preachers can be faithful to our calling and yet remain relevant to our congregations. That path, I suggest, is neither apolitical nor party-political. It is biblical-political.

Before arguing the point, a number of words are in order.

First, a word about the purpose of *Preaching and Politics*. We are living in an era when the secularizing tendencies of the Democratic Party warrant searching and protracted critique.[4] Patrick Hynes articulates the belief of many when he writes:

> Make no mistake, the modern American Left is openly hostile to religion and religious folks who take active roles in politics and public life. That doesn't mean all Democrats are hostile to religion. There are certainly millions of Democrats who are also devout, believing Christians. But too many in the Democratic Party leadership either share this leftist hostility to Americans of faith or are too beholden to leftwing activists to stand up for people of faith when they are under fire.[5]

This critique of the Democratic Party is assumed throughout.

All the same, my goal here is to address preachers of a conservative ilk, who, in occupying their pulpits, tend either to be disengaged from the culture war or embroiled in it beyond the

---

box, for example, voters are forced to decide whether they support a Judeo-Christian view of marriage or wish their tax dollars to go to stem cell research. For Thomas's and Beckel's defining of polarization see *Common Ground*, 3–6, 73–74.

4. Budziszewski writes: "Secularism knows nothing of grace or redemption; it has difficulty speaking of evil; it denies the reality of sin. The heights and the depths are alike unknown to it, and so man is unknown to it. However, imperfect evangelical thought may be, it always remembers both the definition of man and his situation: the image of God, now fallen, but ever sought by his Maker" (*Evangelicals in the Public Square*, 119).

5. Hynes, *In Defense of the Religious Right*, 64.

bounds of their vocation. Whereas the former are hidden away in spiritual ghettos, protesting out of hearing distance the decline of Western society, the latter, frustrated by the way of things and wanting to inject Christian thought and weight into the culture war, have adopted an unself-critical defense of the Republican Party.[6] This tack I perceive to be counterproductive to the longer-term affairs of the kingdom and of the battle for the preservation of Judeo-Christian values in the West.[7] I write primarily then for my own faith community—that is, for those upholding a high (conservative) view of the Bible and of preaching—in the prayerful hope that among the politically conservative a greater objectivity may emerge and the primary biblical focus on the kingdom be kept in view.

My comments about the right and Fox News Channel in particular should not be read then as a free pass for the DNC or for other major TV networks. While admiring Fox News Channel for being right in principle in its defense of traditional values, I am nonetheless concerned by its unreasoning and/or unreasonable conservative elements, and its impact on my own faith community (the Evangelical and specifically Reformed sector of the church).[8] Unself-critical conservatives, I have no doubt, will fail

---

6. Notwithstanding the general alliance between political and theological conservatism, I am mindful of the diversity of political opinion within Evangelicalism (cf. Michael Cromartie's introduction to Budziszewski's *Evangelicals in the Public Square*, 9–10).

7. According to Dinesh D'Souza, we are seeking to preserve these values in the face of folk who are either ignorant of the origins of Western civilization, think they know them, or know them full well but seek to leave them behind (*What's So Great About Christianity?* 41–42).

8. It is interesting that Hillary Clinton and Ed Rendell (Governor of Pennsylvania) both lauded Fox as the most impartial news network of the 2008 presidential campaign. Although their unlikely words of support for Fox are probably the result of the free pass other channels gave Barack Obama, the results of a poll of the Pew Research Center are supportive; namely, that 39 percent of Fox's viewers are currently

to see the value in "objectivizing" their conservatism, when the secularism of much of political liberalism is so pronounced, and in a number of ways so threatening to a Judeo-Christian view of life. Yet, without a more objective approach, conservatives prove to be no better than liberals in the way they argue their case. Their "manufactured outrage" displayed when point-scoring and the double standards often employed, we might expect among non-Christians, but surely disciples of Christ have a divine obligation to be truly "fair and balanced, and unafraid." Indeed, the Word of God, with its revelation of the countercultural standards of Christ's Kingdom, calls us to this objectivism.

Secondly, a word about the focus of *Preaching and Politics*. Central to what follows is not the sprinkling of political comment, but the advocacy of expository preaching. This emphasis is, in itself, apolitical. That said, my transatlantic *sitz-im-Leben* affords me a different perspective on how the expounded Word impacts our Christian understanding of the issues of the present than many single-community Christians may have. I say this neither to boast nor to belittle, only to urge readers to understand the impact of parochialism on thought—a parochialism exacerbated in North America by geographical isolation and the limited availability of truly global news coverage.[9] Writes C. S. Lewis, "A man who has lived in many places is not likely to be deceived by the local errors of his native village."[10] Nor his adopted

---

Republican, 33 percent Democrat and 22 percent Independent. While this does not prove, in my view, that the channel is the most "fair and balanced"—for the poll could suggest simply that Fox's coverage is the most entertaining—I reference the network more than any other because it is the one most relevant to the constituency I wish to address.

9. Americans may rightly or wrongly be critical of the BBC, but it is to the BBC World News that one has to go in America for global news coverage that treats issues on the basis of their inherent importance and not simply because of their relevance to America or to the United Kingdom.

10. C. S. Lewis, *Fern-seed and Elephants*, 35. Along similar lines

village, we may add. Similarly, Lewis continues, "the scholar has lived in many times and is therefore in some degree immune from the great cataract of nonsense that pours from the press and the microphone of his own age."

In my own theological tradition, the parochial spirit tends to assume that anything divergent from the received political conservatism is social liberalism.[11] This assumption appears to be born of a lack of awareness of other styles or types of conservatism found elsewhere than in America. Naturally, Americans have a right to define conservatism appropriate to the States, but it does not follow that any divergence from it is a denial of conservatism, historically defined. Hasty conclusions of denial only succeed in enforcing an impression of parochialism, which in turn raises questions about the credibility of the political conservatism on offer; notably its objectivity, maturity, and security. This sort of conservatism—the conservatism of the blinkered ideologue—is of less than maximal spiritual value in the waging of the present culture war.

In the Christian church an expository approach to preaching is one major way ministers of the Word can encourage better virtues in political discourse, at least among our hearers. One by-product of these virtues is the ability to listen more intently to those we don't necessarily agree with, and to learn from them where we can. Consistent with this, I have drawn on sources that are both leftist and rightist (both politically and theologically). I

Dietrich Bonhoeffer made the comment from prison that change was brought about in his life not by confinement but by his father's personality and by living abroad (*Letters & Papers from Prison*, 88).

11. This observation comports with that of James Q. Wilson, the Ronald Reagan Professor of Public Policy at Pepperdine University. Paraphrasing Wilson's description of political polarization, Thomas and Beckel write, that, "polarization occurs when the opposing camp regards a candidate as not simply wrong, but corrupt and wicked. The assumption is that one side is absolutely right, the other absolutely wrong, and the wrong side deserves to die absolutely" (*Common Ground*, 4).

have done so, practically speaking, because they have been close-at-hand and have helped at various points in the corroboration of my thesis regardless of their standpoint. In utilizing them, I have looked for that which helps the case for the prioritization of the Kingdom of Heaven.

Thirdly, a word about the influences on *Preaching and Politics*. Obviously, this brief study lives in the nexus between Christian theology and politics. It has demanded some insight into the academic contours of both disciplines. What insight there is has come not by intuition. I am glad therefore to acknowledge my debt to the many—first at home and in church, later in high school and university—for the reception of valuable principles about the two arms of God's government: the church and civil authority.

Of the many principles learned domestically, one stands out supremely: my father's advice on leaving home, to follow Christ above and beyond anything and everyone else; distinctively adding, "and that includes me and your mum." My life has been blessed and impoverished according to the degree I have remembered these words. Certainly they have relevance to the "hot potato" handled here. They provide liberty, courage, and focus. I mention them to emphasize that in a climate of much cynicism and distrust, it is my father's advice and not any closet theological or political views that has influenced my line of argument and the decision to publish it.

In thankfulness for the many principles learned in formal education, it is only appropriate to mention the mind-enlarging years of study in the politics department of the University College of Swansea, Wales (1985–88), and at the Free Church of Scotland College, Edinburgh (1989–93). Besides learning much about political history and ideology as well as Christian history, theology, and praxis, I received training in the use of the mind; not least its powers for critical analysis. This training has been put to use since in the exciting challenge of academic research at the Universities of Edinburgh and Tübingen, as well as in the weekly blessing of biblical exposition and pastoral counsel. It has afforded me a vocational outlet in which to follow my father's advice. The result has been an independence in Christ of both mind and action.[12]

This independence does not sit well with everyone, and, applied to the arena of politics, there is a sense in which it does not sit well with me either. It would suit my yearning for straightforwardness to claim that Scripture provides the theological blueprint for one mainstream political ideology and party manifesto over another. But it does not completely, no matter the lengths some go to in order to claim that it does. The sweeping dismissal of nuanced thinking as "flip-flopping" is itself unconvincing and sometimes disingenuous. Our fallen scenario simply does not allow for such simplicity, nor does the experience of international living.

It is as a citizen of the United Kingdom and as a permanent resident of the United States that I write. These countries—one by birth and the other by adoption—I love, not least for their God-given freedoms that afford the opportunity for public discussion of what is for their best. But the perspective I bring is an objective one forged by my migrant experience—first as a newcomer to America and now, coming on the tenth anniversary of my arrival in the United States, as a transatlantic visitor to my native Britain. I would not trade this objectivity, no matter how much it leaves me open to misunderstanding.[13] But two things I ask. First, that it not be taken for an unappreciative deprecation of either the United Kingdom or the United States. God has

---

12. My personal story here resonates the truth of Karl Barth's comment that, "the independence of preaching does not rule out theological apprenticeship." He continues: "A theological student . . . is one who has been taught by teachers to walk on his own and to handle scripture independently" (*Homiletics*, 83–84).

13. On the possibilities of being misunderstood, see Thomas and Dobson, *Blinded by Might*, 7–8.

greatly blessed these lands. My purpose in writing is not to deny this fact, but to ask what we have been doing with these blessings. Secondly, I ask that my objectivity not be dismissed as a distorted independence—a sort of egotistical isolationism. It is rather a readiness to submit to the authority and scope of God's Word in its teaching and application, no matter how inconvenient this submission may be to me or to you.

My overall concern, then, is spiritual not material. History teaches us that when we get our spiritual priorities right, general advantages follow. As a wise man put it long ago: "Righteousness exalts a nation, but sin is a reproach to any people" (Prov 14:34). I thank God for planting my feet in two nations that have known this truth and for the opportunity, in this small way, to keep this principle alive today. Many readers may take umbrage with this or that, but I pray that many more will warm to the thought shared here that one day there will be but one victor on the battlefield of time. His name is Jesus (Phil 2:9–10). Given this, should not we preachers enlist for battle in the present culture war, but insist when doing so that we use his anointed weapons and tactics rather than our own?

Fourthly, a word about the hope of *Preaching and Politics*. By means of it I attempt in some modest way to urge the reestablishment of Jesus' prioritization of his Kingdom in the minds of God's people. The more I have thought and now written about this the more I have found others to share the same burden. Indeed, in looking for corroboration of my argument, I discovered that authors such as Charles Colson, Cal Thomas, and Ed Dobson, have aired similar thoughts before me.[14] Far from dissuading

---

14. I refer to Thomas's and Beckel's *Common Ground*, Thomas's and Dobson's *Blinded by Might*, and Charles Colson's *God & Government*. I have found them to express very well in general what I am trying to say of pulpit ministry in particular. Jim Wallis's *God's Politics* also has much to say that is relevant. In the throes of pastoral ministry it has not proven possible to do justice to Wallis's work. Accordingly, I have left reference to his work to a later opportunity. The same goes for the briefer

me from continuing, their insights spurred me on to proceed to publication. First, because it appears the church is slow to learn the lessons these brothers have taught. Second, because however history judges the Bush 43 Presidency—and I hope he gets a fairer judgment from posterity—the past eight years have revealed the challenges of the faithful in politics. Third, because whereas my brothers have dealt more generally with the question of the Christian approach to politics, my contribution looks more specifically at the role of the preacher or minister.[15] I put it to you that in the theological and specifically Christian realm there is need of an ecclesial version of the "radical middle."[16] In the pews, this radical middle stands between the radical right and the radical left, but in the pulpits it stands between attitudes toward the culture war of nonengagement and over-engagement. The radical middle, known throughout the study as the biblical-political approach, speaks of an authentic engagement in the politics of the day, yet one that is without compromise.

The endeavor to depict and to uphold a balanced approach is a hard enough task, but will remain all the more so as long as the Democratic Party remains so beholden to secular progressives. All the same, there are efforts that can and ought to be made to challenge, where legitimate, the partisanship that has invaded the church. If Thomas and Beckel are right, that "polarization's domination over politics is coming to an end,"[17] it makes good sense to

---

comment found in David Kinnaman's and Gabe Lyons's *unChristian*.

15. The work of the preacher is, of course, implied by these brothers, and sometimes spoken of directly. See, for example, Ed Dobson's testimony in *Blinded by Might*, 155ff.

16. Thomas and Beckel, *Common Ground*, 36. The term "radical middle" is descriptive of those reconsidering the views of the "radical right" and "radical left."

17. Thomas and Beckel, *Common Ground*, 11. They continue: "We believe that the glory days of the braying radio hosts and mudslinging political consultants are numbered. So, too, the propagandists, who hide out in 'think tanks' underwritten by wealthy extremists who get a tax

work for the same in the church. Indeed, having initially intended the publication of *Preaching and Politics* in time for the 2008 Presidential race, it now appears to be a godsend that the study is going to publication at the outset of what is clearly a new chapter in American political history. The country is rethinking some things. It is evident the church is in need of doing so as well.

In going public with *Preaching and Politics*, I thank those many congregations that have been such a blessing to me over the years. In one way or another they have helped to shape my thinking and my life. The Welsh congregations in which I grew up exercised a formative influence. I think most warmly of the good folk of Bethany Evangelical Church, Clarbeston Road, Pembrokeshire; Holywell Evangelical Church and Flint Evangelical Church, both in North-East Wales. Then there are those congregations that were such a blessing to me during my student days: Ebenezer Baptist Church, Swansea; Buccleuch and Greyfriars Free Church of Scotland, Edinburgh; Grove Chapel, Camberwell, London; and Durham Presbyterian Church, Co. Durham. In America, Cornerstone Church of Skippack and Central Schwenkfelder Church, Worcester Township, Pennsylvania, have been such wonderful examples of the love of Christ. Since June 2007, it has been my daily privilege to work with the Consistory, staff, and congregation of Seventh Reformed Church, Grand Rapids, Michigan. They, together with dear friends in the city, plus our radio listeners, have proven to be a constant source of encouragement, stimuli, love, and support. Philippians 1:3!

I am specifically indebted to a number of friends and colleagues who either read the manuscript at various stages or who sharpened my thinking: John Armstrong, Cindy Freeman, William Tuinstra, and especially Elsa Baker and Marilyn Van Dyke (Copy Editor).

For the second time, I am indebted to the staff of Wipf and Stock; on this occasion to Jim Tedrick (Managing Editor),

---

deduction for demeaning the political process."

Christian Amondson (Assistant Managing Editor), and Tina Campbell Owens (typesetter) especially. It is a privilege to work with a publisher that puts such store by the value of ideas. Which reminds me to say, and sincerely so, that mention of these good folk does not implicate them in any of the opinions I offer, or in any errors of my argument.

Speaking of which, there is one opinion that some readers may find especially problematic. It is implied by the pronoun "he," used in reference to "the preacher," and discloses that, to date, I have found unconvincing overall the exegetical, hermeneutical, and pragmatic arguments in favor of the ordination of women. This admission does not imply any obsession with the issue, nor any animosity toward female clergy. Some I have known (and know) as dear friends, and some I have worked with as colleagues in various capacities (most recently on TCT.TV's "Ask the Pastor" program). I merely take a different standpoint on the scriptural information available. In doing so, I am very thankful for every influence in my life that has taught me to distinguish issues from people.

Others may agree with the principles expounded, but disagree with the political illustrations used. If you find this to be the case, may I ask that you not allow the illustrations to turn you off to the principles? Whereas the illustrations are of passing relevance; the principles, if scriptural, are abiding, and therefore are more important. May God help us to embrace them and to work them out heartily! The honor of Christ and the welfare and growth of his Kingdom is at stake.

Dr. Tim J. R. Trumper,
Seventh Reformed Church,
Grand Rapids, Michigan
www.7thref.org

1

A Middle Way

The Method of the Biblical-Political Approach

If Christ is the Saviour of the world, then politics, too, can be saved, that is, it can be penetrated and quickened by the grace of Christ....

—Jacques Maritain,
The Twilight of Civilization

THIS IS the age of 24/7 global news coverage. It gives us immediate exposure to much that is of concern, whether it be the war on terror—what Newt Gingrich describes as the beginning of World War III—or the internecine conflict raging in the West between liberals and conservatives over Judeo-Christian values.[1] These tensions significantly challenge all Christians, not least preachers who are divinely charged with interpreting earthly affairs by means of the heavenly perspective.[2] As indi-

---

1. For a sympathetic history of the secularization that spawned the battle between liberals and conservatives, see Wilson's *God's Funeral*. While much of this history has to do with Europe—notably the spiritual decline of England from the seventeenth-century (the "heyday of the English sermon") to the present, wherein "the English have lost any sense of what religion is" (Paxman, *The English*, 105, 112)—it sheds significant light on the American context.

2. The focus on pulpit ministry explains the predominant concern in

viduals we preachers are entitled to our own political opinions, and many of us hold them strongly. But this does not answer the question as to whether our public service should be politically free or politically charged. The view put forward here — based on an appreciation of the importance of expository preaching and personal transatlantic observations of the church's response to the sociopolitical challenges of the day—is that we ministers ought not to preach more narrowly (i.e., apolitically) than Christ would wish, nor more broadly (i.e., party-politically).[3] Stated otherwise, we ought to be neither "politically celibate"[4] nor more akin to the political ideologue or propagandist. Rather, we must speak biblically-politically.

1. THE APOLITICAL APPROACH

Characteristic of the apolitical approach is a reticence to speak in detail of the deteriorating social, cultural, and political situation of the day. Preachers of this outlook may have a high view of Scripture, but express this reticence by curtailing the scope of the teaching and application of Scripture to issues that are distinctively and exclusively spiritual. This narrowing of the content of preaching is achieved either by forgoing the consecutive exposition of the Word in favor of a diet of individual texts, by hyper-spiritualizing its content, or by refusing to follow

---

the following chapters with special revelation. We shall touch briefly in chapter three on the use of general revelation, but chiefly as it relates to the witness and work of those to whom we minister.

3. I have found welcome support for these observations from John Stott, *I Believe in Preaching*, 159–73; Lord Blanch of Bishopthorpe, "Is There any Word from the Lord?" 80–98; and Campolo, *Is Jesus a Republican or a Democrat?* esp. 1–16). Stott in particular takes a very similar line and for the same reason: the protection and promotion of expository preaching.

4. Michael Cromartie's introduction to Budziszewski's *Evangelicals in the Public Square*, 10.

through on certain more sensitive or controversial implications of Scripture. The obvious result is that he has no audible voice in the culture war.

This reticence is not new. It seems to me to have been the default position of many a conservative preacher in England and Wales for some time now. The position is born—ironically in the British scene given the connectedness of the church and the state—of a dualistic separation of the secular and the sacred. It issues in an ignoring of the reality of the prevailing situation, in the belief that preachers must engage spiritual issues alone.[5] Martin Niemöller's *Dachau Sermons* forcibly indict this belief:

> The type of Christianity which isolates itself, which allows the wicked world to follow its course, and is content

---

5. Half a century ago, French political philosopher Jacques Maritain (1882–1973) complained that

> ... one of the most deep-seated vices of the modern world has been its dualism, its disassociation of the things of God from the things of the world. The latter, the appurtenances of social, economic and political life, have been abandoned to their proper carnal law and divorced from the exigencies of the Gospel. The result is that they have become more and more unlivable. At the same time, Christian morality, no longer vitalizing the social life of nations, has become, in this respect, a universe of worlds and formulas, not intrinsically, nor in the Church, but rather in the world, in the general public behaviour of culture. And there, in this practical behaviour of civilization, such a universe of words and formulas has found itself effectively vassalized by temporal activities which are really quite detached from Christ. This kind of disorder cannot be cured except by the renewal of the most profound energies of the religious conscience surging up into temporal existence (*The Twilight of Civilization*, 25).

to hope for a better hereafter, is nothing but a caricature, a foolish cartoon. The terrestrial life of Jesus himself, as also the activity of his apostles, proves it by showing how the Gospel is a power of God which constantly urges forward to action, to work while it is still day.[6]

The apolitical preacher's rallying cry "Just preach the gospel!" sounds worthy enough. Often the cry has in view, however, but the gospel's narrower and more individualistic application: the redemption of the individual at the expense of society or the cosmos (Rom 8:22–3). The approach is regularly accompanied by a retreat into individualistic pietism. Furthermore, it includes a worthy stress on society's need for a widespread spiritual awakening, but too often emphasizes the need for an extraordinary operation of the Holy Spirit at the expense of his everyday operations. Moreover, it ignores the calls evangelical revivals made for social action.[7] Accordingly, the apolitical approach subtly dissuades Christians from speaking up proactively about society's ills, other than in the most overt terms of the gospel (narrowly defined). Sometimes this dissuasion is rooted in the rightful belief that only the gospel can save society, but there are occasions when the apolitical approach comes across as a veil obscuring a loss of hope, faith even, amid the overwhelming odds facing the church. In such cases, the call for revival—for God to work—can substitute for a readiness in ourselves to battle for the hearts and minds of our peers.[8] Rightly, John Stott calls this approach "irresponsible":

> Christian people are crying out for guidance in these areas [that is, the social, moral, and political implications of the faith]. They want to be helped to think about them

---

6. Niemöller, *Dachau Sermons*, 33.

7. Schaeffer, *A Christian Manifesto* in *The Complete Works*, 5:451–52.

8. See the comments of D. M. Lloyd-Jones on avoiding warfare in "The Weapons of Our Warfare," 202–3.

as Christians. Shall we abandon them to swim in these deep waters alone? This is the way of the coward.[9]

The result has been disastrous. "Most Christians...," to quote Dinesh D'Souza,

> have retreated into a Christian subculture where they engage Christian concerns. Then they step back into secular society, where their Christianity is kept out of sight until the next church service. Without realizing it Christians have become postmodernists of a sort: they live by the gospel of the two truths. There is religious truth, reserved for Sundays and days of worship, and there is secular truth, which applies to the rest of the time.[10]

One of the purposes of going into print is to challenge this retreat from civic engagement.[11] Ray Pennings of the Work Research Foundation, Canada, draws our attention to the ex-

---

9. Stott, *I Believe in Preaching*, 169.
10. D'Souza, *What's So Great About Christianity?* xiv.
11. Writes Colson:
    Christian values are in retreat in the West today, primarily, I believe, because of the church itself. If Christianity has failed to stem the rising tides of relativism it is because the church in many instances has lost the convicting force of the gospel message ... while humanists did not understand humans, Christians did not understand Christianity. This is surely evident in post- World-War-II Christianity, which has become a religion of private comfort and blessing that fills up whatever small holes in life that pleasure, money, and success have left open, what Bonhoeffer called a "god of the gaps" (*God & Government*, 252).

The context of *God & Government* reminds us, however, that the gospel message the church has lost the conviction of is not only the narrow message of the apolitical but the more comprehensive gospel of the biblical-political (see below).

ample of well-known church leader John MacArthur. According to Pennings, MacArthur opposes political activism because it denigrates the sovereignty of God over history and its events; it promotes within culture biblical values by carnal means; it creates a false sense of morality; and risks alienating unbelievers by casting them as political enemies rather than as a mission field.[12] Allowing for MacArthur's understandable reaction to the stridency of political conduct today, and upholding MacArthur's underlying desire to uphold the spirituality of Christian living and service, Pennings nevertheless concludes that "to discourage any form of civic involvement . . . is to depart from a rich Reformed heritage."[13] With this I agree, and for reasons that will become apparent in what follows.

2. THE PARTY-POLITICAL APPROACH

Alternatively, those utilizing the partisan approach frequently substitute addresses on relevant historico-political/party-political topics for the exposition of the Word. They forget, in the words of Karl Barth, that "preaching must not be a welling up of our own speech. In both form and content it must be exposition of scripture."[14] I recall, for example, reading a most fascinating autobiographical sketch by Ian R. K. Paisley, founder of Free

12. Pennings, "Political Ministers of God," 365.

13. Ibid.

14. Barth, *Homiletics*, 88. In relation to expository preaching Barth writes:
> I have not to talk *about* scripture but *from* it. I have not to say something, but merely to repeat something. If God alone wants to speak in a sermon, neither theme nor *scopus* should get in the way. . . . Our task is simply to follow the distinctive movement of thought in the text, to stay with this, and not with a plan that arises out of it (Ibid., 49).

Presbyterianism in Northern Ireland, and, until recently, the undisputed leader of the province's Unionism. Gripped by the account I was nevertheless left with a nagging doubt as to whether the pulpit is the place for the "four windows" on his remarkable life.[15] Likewise there come to mind those (often televised) "sermons" of the admirable figure, the late D. James Kennedy, which deal with topics such as the Christian roots of America and the history of evolution.[16]

In questioning approaches like these, I am not saying that there is never a place for topical preaching. In fact there are occasions when it would be unwise, even inappropriate, not to break

---

15. My particular criticism of Dr. Paisley ought not to be lumped with that easy and blanket criticism lodged from mainland Britain, often by Christians hidden away in apolitical bunkers. Whatever significant methodological issues his work has raised, especially during his tenure as First Minister (a post that cost him his Moderatorship of the Free Presbyterian Church), the nature of Northern Ireland's troubles cautions us against too severe a judgment. Few who criticize him for excessive involvement in politics can legitimately claim to have been as active evangelistically. See Rhonda Paisley's portrait of her father in *Ian Paisley*, 118–28 especially. My own father's ministerial connections to Dr. Paisley afford me a close-at-hand awareness of the importance he has placed on the gospel and evangelism.

16. Again, my questioning of those sermons of Dr. Kennedy more historical, political or social in nature should not be interpreted as a dismissal of his life's active and noteworthy concern for country. I challenge not the establishment of the Center for Reclaiming America or the D. James Kennedy Center for Christian Statesmanship, simply his substitution of addresses on national concerns for the exposition of the Word in Lord's Day worship.

Take, for instance, Kennedy's 1997 Memorial Day sermon "Will the Church Forget?" based on Matt 22:21: "Render therefore unto Caesar the things that are Caesar's; and unto God the things that are God's" (KJV). While full of passion in urging pastors to speak out on the issues of the day, the sermon entirely lacks exegesis and exposition. Accordingly, the sermon says less than it could, and has the feel of the authority of a great man rather than that of a great God (Kennedy, *Will the Church Forget?*).

off from a series of expository sermons.[17] But when we do so, we are still bound to use Scripture as fully and as faithfully as we can. A topical sermon must still be a sermon, and can still maintain to a significant degree exegetical and expository qualities.

With the intensification of the present culture war, it seems the party-political approach has been gaining ground, not least in America. Most preachers, alert to the likelihood "the West is passing away" (to use Pat Buchanan's phrase),[18] and fearing for the future of traditional Judeo-Christian values, have taken to the public square in order to demand a hearing.[19] These concerns are valid and most worthy of outspokenness. My argument for the biblical-political approach should not be seen to mute this concern in the slightest. What is troubling, however, is the route party-political preachers have taken over recent decades to address them. Writes John W. Whitehead of the Rutherford Institute: "Modern Christianity, having lost sight of Christ's teachings, has been co-opted by legalism, materialism and politics. Put simply, it has lost its spirituality."[20] An evidence of this is the transfer of hope from the power of the gospel to the efficiency of party machinery. Accordingly, preachers have promoted increasingly one political party over another, and expected their hearers to vote accordingly. Whereas African-American congregations generally follow their leadership and vote Democratic, in many

17. To have continued an expository series the first Sunday after 9/11 with a passage of no relevance to the happenings of the previous week would, for example, have bordered on the ridiculous—an insensitivity to the congregants' needs amounting to negligence.

18. Heard of on "Hannity and Colmes," Fox News, August 22, 2006. The phrase is taken from Buchanan's book, *State of Emergency*.

19. Campolo, *Is Jesus a Republican or a Democrat?* xvii. Recently thirty pastors located across numerous American states illustrated this increasing partisanship by using their "Pulpit Freedom Sunday" (September 28, 2008) to challenge a fifty-four-year-old law granting churches tax exempt status on condition of nonpartisan pulpit usage.

20. Cited by David Kuo in "Putting Faith Before Politics."

a conservative Euro-American congregation it is a brave person who confesses to voting likewise.[21]

While this partisan approach is made understandable in many ways by the secularization of the Democratic Party and is warranted in principle to the degree that it challenges the lopsided spirituality of the apolitical, I fear it is taken too far. In the opinion of James Bopp, "Pastors, as individuals, have the same rights as all other American citizens to involve themselves in political activity. Pastors thus have much greater latitude to involve themselves in political activities than does a church."[22] I argue, however, that having the right to be politically active (in a party-political sense) does not mean that it is wise for preachers to take advantage of it. There is a cost to our calling, and wisely refraining from involvement in *party-political* activities (outside of extreme circumstances) is, it seems to me, part of that cost. Not only is it uncertain whether a preacher can ordinarily be involved party-politically without implicating the congregation he serves, his involvement could lead him away from the true nature of his calling.[23] Party-political activism could well leave him dancing precariously along the fine, sometimes invisible, line distinguishing the Lord's agenda from his own (be it Republican or Democrat [U.S.], Labour, Conservative, or Liberal Democrat [U.K.]). Indeed, the pitfalls of the party-political preacher were amply illustrated during the 2008 presidential race.

21. For all the Democrats' excitement that nearly 30 percent of white evangelicals ("the true Republican base") voted Democratic in the 2006 elections—up from 22 percent in the 2004 Presidential election (an "aberrantly low" figure)—David Kuo claims that Democrats would be unwise to rethink their public policy agenda in hopes of attracting evangelicals. His argument is that evangelicals are reexamining their spiritual and not their political priorities (Ibid.).

22. Bopp, "Do's and Don'ts for Political Activities for Pastors."

23. Bopp makes no clear statement as to whether he thinks the endorsement of a candidate from the pulpit would be seen in the eyes of the law as a personal or a church endorsement of a candidate or party (Ibid.).

On the Democratic side, there were the antics of Rev. Jeremiah Wright of Trinity United Church of Christ, Chicago. For those of us outside the circles of Black Nationalism, and less influenced by Liberation theology, some of Dr. Wright's statements have been truly astounding, as have those of his Roman Catholic friend Rev. Michael Pfleger. In an age in which the (right-wing) media has made criticism of America tantamount to a lack of patriotism, these men of the cloth have undoubtedly hit on a real but unpalatable truth; namely that there is sin in American history and society. This fact no amount of patriotism can alter, nor can the (right-wing) media's focus *ad nauseam* on their extremes. Nonetheless, the absurdities of Wright's claims—not least the government's supposed invention of aids to destroy the African-American community—has brought pulpit ministry into disrepute. Nothing has perhaps summed up the problems of Wright's approach more than his rant "God damn America." The sin in this rant, assuming it was reported fairly, is not its failure to square with the blindly patriotic and naively unqualified mantra "God bless America," but its withholding from Americans the hope of Christ.[24] The rant as it stands is devoid of the gospel.

24. There are two problems with the mantra "God bless America." First, it expresses an implicit universalism, the spirit of which John McCain articulated in his 2008 Convention speech receiving the Republican Presidential nomination: "We're all the children of God; we're all Americans." Secondly, it helps unbelievers ignore the fact that God's richest blessings come via atonement and the gifts of repentance and faith. Many doubtless mean the mantra well, but there are always those who hope for God's blessing in the face of their disregard for his Word and Law. We thus need to distinguish constructive criticism of America—sympathetic-critical criticism if you like, which is aimed at building up the country—from that destructive pulling down of the "Great Republic" (an allusion to Sir Winston Churchill's tome *The Great Republic*).

Over against the left- and right-wing extremes of "God damn America" and "God bless America" is the true Christian response: "God redeem America." This alternative makes better theology and pulpit oratory, in that it captures both the reality of the human condition and

On the Republican side, some significant voices have been lost of late by death. I think of Jerry Falwell (1933–2007) and James Kennedy (1930–2007), two significant influences in the formation of the Moral Majority.[25] Nonetheless, the 2008 race witnessed the spectacle of Pastor John Hagee publicly endorsing John McCain, only to retract some of his comments about the Roman Catholic Church under the pressure of the media. It does not concern us here whether Hagee's view of the Catholic Church as "the Great Whore" was right or wrong. What is of interest is that his endorsement of a *political* campaign led to his retraction of a *theological* viewpoint, notwithstanding the fact he is a preacher and not a politician. This brings into question the legitimacy of preachers endorsing party-political candidates. The episode also raises questions about Hagee's theological convictions. Why did he not rather retract his endorsement and maintain his conviction, if that is what he genuinely believed about the Roman Catholic Church? Only Rev. Hagee knows whether his retraction was an act of humility or a pragmatic prioritizing of his endorsement. All the same, the retraction indicates that his ministerial calling took a back-seat at that point to his interest in influencing, along party-political and candidate-specific lines, the race for the White House. Hagee thus seems to lend weight, in part at least, to Gordon MacDonald's observation of the:

---

the hope of the gospel. It also resonates a truer patriotism, one that is loyal but not blind, and understands that God's richest blessings are entitlements of grace rather than nationality. See Appendix A for a good example of this patriotism.

25. For a brief history of Falwell's political involvement, see Thomas and Beckel, *Common Ground*, 105–8. Tracing Falwell's 180-degree turn from an apolitical to a party-political stance, Thomas and Beckel conclude that "His legacy will not be in politics but his university and the people he introduced to God through his pastoral ministry." For a fuller history and assessment of the Moral Majority, see Thomas's and Dobson's *Blinded by Might*, passim.

> hints that the movement [Evangelicalism]—once cobbled together by Billy Graham and Harold Ockenga—is beginning to fragment because it is more identified by a political agenda that seems to be failing and less identified by a commitment to Jesus and his kingdom.[26]

The patriotism which instills fear in the party-political preacher that his country is going to the dogs is no doubt honorable, but this does not mean to say that Christ's pulpits are the place from which to sound a politically partisan alarm. As MacDonald notes, we have a greater Kingdom to put first.

3. THE BIBLICAL-POLITICAL APPROACH

The drawbacks of the apolitical and party-political approaches call for a third option, one that mediates between them and does so because it actually has the best biblical credentials. Outworked through expository preaching, the biblical-political approach maximizes the importance and pursuit of the truth relevant to the church and to society. If the Bible supplies more politically relevant information than the apolitical with their narrow soteric and pietistic concerns might imagine, it stops well short of either certifying the credentials of any given political system (certainly biblically incompatible systems such as Fascism and Communism), or of serving as a party-political document or handbook.[27] Somewhere in between there lies a path that may be trodden toward a balanced utilization of the Bible that is cultur-

---

26. MacDonald, "Leader's Insight," 4.

27. Sometimes Christian political participants are honest enough to admit this. For example, erstwhile British Labour politician Paul Boateng (currently British High Commissioner to South Africa) writes: "Anyone looking to the Gospels . . . for a simple endorsement of a set of political prescriptions or the ultimate in Labour party political manifestos of yesteryear, long on prose and short on practicalities, will be disappointed." ("The Hope of Things to Come," 53).

ally and politically relevant, but is underpinned by the treatment of the Bible on its own terms.

By committing ourselves to the fulsome exposition of the Word, we preachers avoid the apolitical narrowing of Scripture's teaching and application, as well as the party-political "terrestrialization" of its meaning. In doing so, we refuse to be either silent about politics or dominated by them.[28] It is God's Word that shapes our comment and not, typically, the events that are political. As Campolo writes, God:

> . . . stands above all political parties and calls each of them into judgment. Likewise, He calls upon us to rise above all of this, and He expects us to use the Scriptures as a touchstone to test whether the policies and practices of political parties are in harmony with His will. God expects us never to let partisan loyalty tempt us into reading the platform ideas of any party into the Bible. If we are to be faithful to the true God, we must not allow the principles of any party to override what the Bible has to say to us.[29]

Thus, while the biblical-political preacher has, as part of his calling, to be something of a political analyst—as much of one as the party-political preacher—he will never forget that he is first and foremost a proclaimer of the Word. Indeed, the intent behind his political analysis is driven by the need to discover or to discern how the Word applies in the present situation.

This interest in balance arises from a concern that the lopsided apolitical and party-political alternatives are currently winning out.[30] These extremes of pulpit use have been possible

---

28. In the words of the nineteenth-century Bishop of Liverpool, J. C. Ryle, "we are to observe carefully the public events of the times in which we live. We are not to be absorbed in politics, but we are to mark political events" (*Expository Thoughts on Luke*, 2:377).

29. Campolo, *Is Jesus a Republican or a Democrat?* 3.

30. The demise of polarization in the political realm that Thomas

I suggest, because expository preaching—so critical to the biblical-political conveyance of the scriptural world-and-life view—has not held the place it merits in the pulpits of the church. This biblical-political (expository) approach enables ministers of the Word to address the current climate in a relevant manner, while nevertheless seeking to ensure that what we say resonates with the will of Christ our King. After all, it is his Kingdom we are called to proclaim.

Although the nomenclature "biblical-political" may be new, the approach to the nexus between the pulpit and politics is not. The increasing reflection of the tenor of society's political divisions within the church (especially in America)—notably their poison and politics of personal destruction—warrants its fresh presentation. This "third way" is, says Stott, "brave not cowardly, humble not dogmatic, and prudent not foolish."[31] While it utilizes what is best from the apolitical and party-political approaches, it is servant to neither. Sharing the party-political insistence on addressing the social, political, and religious questions of the day, it nevertheless appreciates the apolitical concern to maintain the spiritual character of the preacher's calling. Maritain sums up the point well:

> When we say that Christendom must be made anew by Christian means or perish completely; that there is no good to be expected from political undertakings of violence and regimentation, or of self-styled Christian totalitarianism, animated as they are by the very spirit which is the prime source of the evils from which civilization is suffering today; and that the persevering and patient action and the manifestation of the Christian spirit in the world are more important than the external

---

and Beckel speak of has yet to encourage apolitical preachers toward a greater biblical responsiveness to the culture war, or to persuade party-political preachers to rethink their heavily partisan response.

31. Stott, *I Believe in Preaching*, 169.

apparatus of a Christian order: we are merely asserting that the principle of the primacy of the spiritual has to be respected even in the manner in which we shall work to bring it into existence; that the primacy of the spiritual, in other words, cannot be brought about by a negation of itself.[32]

This "primacy of the spiritual" is precisely the strength of the biblical-political approach. The better we utilize it the more we shall exceed the apolitical in contributing to the holistic redemption of society; and the less likely we shall be to negate the uniqueness of ministry through the party-political adoption of inappropriate strategies.[33] The following chapters go some way to explain the confidence of this assertion.

---

32. Maritain, *The Twilight of Civilization*, 27.

33. The chart in Appendix B containing the methodological differences between preachers that are apolitical, party-political, and biblical-political serves as a brief summary of the present chapter useful for the understanding of ch. 2.

STUDY QUESTIONS[34]

1. Do you understand your ministry of the Word/the ministry of your pastor to be apolitical, party-political, or biblical-political; or perhaps a mixture of these different approaches? What features of the preaching bring you to your conclusion?

2. Can you justify biblically your understanding of the nexus between preaching and politics?

3. What positive and/or negative effects have you seen as a result of your/your minister's approach? What measure of pragmatism governs your reaction to the perceived effects?

4. What improvements to your/your minister's preaching are necessary and possible for the engagement of the culture war without the compromise of calling?

---

34. While the book is written largely for ministers of the Word, the questions are framed in such a way as to ensure their relevance for all readers and study groups.

2

A Spiritual Way

The Propriety of the Biblical-Political Approach

I believe that the Scriptures provide a valuable source of argument, reflection and aspiration which is not irrelevant to the issues which dominate and disturb Western society. We must not be deterred by the distance in time and space of these ancient writings. Whatever our private attitudes to them may be, they are the product of the Judeo-Christian tradition which has been hugely influential in the forming of our public institutions, our educational practice, our underlying attitudes to life.

—Lord Blanch of Bishopthorpe,
Christianity & Conservatism

If the biblical-political preacher's approach to the culture war entails the prioritization of the Word, his utilization of it demonstrates the propriety of his approach. We see this in numerous ways, not least in:

1. THE SAFEGUARDING OF THE SANCTITY OF DIVINE WORSHIP

There is some common ground between the biblical-political and apolitical approaches when it comes to the important matter of public worship. Preachers of both methods understand that its safeguarding is a must no matter how pressing the issues of the day. They appreciate that worship is by definition heaven-centered, and to be preserved from a lopsided immanence; that is, from a transcendent-less embroilment with earthly affairs. Consistent with this, we ensure that it is God who through Scripture sets the worship agenda, and not the events that are current. This means that the sermon, which is the pinnacle of worship, is to derive its content from Scripture. Only in this way can we ensure that God is "allowed" to speak for himself. Spirit-aided exegesis, hermeneutics (interpretation), and delivery grant his voice the outlet he has ordained. Accordingly, in the sermon we hear not a would-be Bill O'Reilly or Chris Matthews, a John Gibson or a Lou Dobbs (U.S.), a Jeremy Paxman or Kirsty Wark (U.K.), as in the case of the party-political preacher, but almighty God speaking through the human instrument he himself has chosen and equipped to speak from Scripture into the present situation. In the course of preaching, the servant of God can pass relevant political comment, but he takes his cue from Scripture.[1] Only after laying a solid foundation of exposition does he look to bridge the gap between the ancient text and the (post)modern context. In this way he ensures that what he says by way of application is correlative to the meaning of the text or passage in view, and is therefore faithful to it.

---

1. In terms of the law, "a church or pastor is free to state the position of a candidate on any issue and may comment on that position (including praise or criticizing the candidate for it)" (Bopp, "Do's and Don'ts for Political Activities of Pastors").

2. THE MAINTAINING OF A HIGH VIEW OF PREACHING

Approaches to preaching are many and varied. The following predominate in many areas of the church, certainly in her Evangelical and Reformed constituencies:[2]

- Anecdotal preaching: an approach relying on the better known/more easily accessible passages of Scripture, which often takes but soundbites from them as a means of maximizing the application and relevance of Scripture. This approach can serve the purposes of either the apolitical (with their narrow emphasis on devotion and spirituality) or the party-political (with their concern to get to the political punchline).

- Doctrinaire preaching: an approach purporting to be biblical, but too often guilty of imposing on Scripture a theological framework decided not so much by exegesis as by the contours of systematic theology.[3] On this under-

---

2. In the approaches enumerated here I have limited my comment to those that bear on the entirety of Scripture. Accordingly, I have omitted reference to biographical preaching (preaching that traces the stories of particular biblical characters), evangelistic preaching (preaching that emphasizes the winning of the lost to Christ), and experimental or experiential preaching (preaching that tests living and experience by the Word of God). These may be included in one way and/or another within the overall anecdotal, doctrinaire, expository, redemptive-historical, and topical approaches to pulpit ministry.

3. While it is "the system of truth that elucidates each text [of Scripture]," the control of systematic theology is subject to certain qualifications or rules: (1) no doctrine is to be built on a single passage; (2) no doctrine should suppress the force of a given text or passage in the interests of the overall system of theology; (3) the text or passage should not be co-opted for the defense of the system unless its exegesis naturally points in this direction; (4) no sermon should try to bring out all that systematic theology has to say of the doctrine(s) in a given

standing, preaching becomes the practice of demonstrating and defending the framework or the system. Although a longstanding historical approach, Catechetical preaching is in principle an example of this doctrinaire homiletic. Not only does it implicitly challenge the supremacy of the Word of God, it does insufficient justice to the varied genre of Scripture (expressive of its humanness). Resonating a high view of Scripture, doctrinaire preaching nevertheless promotes a lower use of it. With its inordinate focus on theology (i.e., its emphasis on doctrinal propositions, frequently at the expense of Scripture's application), doctrinaire preaching can almost exclusively be found among the apolitical. Preachers of a partisan inclination are simply too politically oriented to have much patience with the overt theological concerns of the doctrinaire.

- Exegetical or Expository preaching: an exegetically based approach to exposition that is sensitive to differences between the Old and New Testaments, to the various genres of literature within each, to the authorial diversity of Scripture (especially relevant in New Testament exposition), and to the need for application that accords with the principles of any given text or passage. Exegetical or expository preaching is distinguished from doctrinaire preaching by the refusal of the expositor to allow dogmatics to overshadow the text. Writes Macleod, "The text itself will normally provide not only the theme but also the divisions of the sermon . . . . It will also provide momentum, as we move through the successive phases of its teaching."[4] Moreover, expository preaching does greater justice to the context of the passage at hand and the life-situation to which it is applied. Continues Macleod:

---

text or passage, (based on Donald Macleod's thought in "Preaching and Systematic Theology," 248–53).

4. Macleod, "Preaching and Systematic Theology," 253–54.

> To abstract the text from its existential setting in Scripture and impose on it instead the dynamics of mere literary style (alliteration) or of dogmatics is not only to jeopardize the liveliness and the relevance of our preaching, but to abandon the role of expositors. We must be faithful not only to the doctrines of the text but to the pastoral perspective that underlies it.

Noting that the core of expository preaching is the style and content of a particular sermon—the *esse* of preaching entailing the unfolding of the meaning and significance of the text or passage in view—Sinclair Ferguson nevertheless reminds us of the importance of systematic or consecutive exposition. This he describes as the *bene esse* of preaching. "Such are its advantages," he writes, "that it ought to be the staple (if not exclusive) diet of the preacher's ministry."[5] For it affords not only a better understanding of the Word, but also a better knowledge of how to read it.

- Redemptive-historical preaching: preaching that considers any given text within the broader biblical context of the history of salvation. Often mistaken as the true homiletical application of biblical theology, it underplays the fact that not all of Scripture is set within a clear redemptive-historical trajectory. More relevant to the present study is the comment of theologian John Frame. Redemptive-historical preaching, he explains,

  > ... focuses on the historical narrative of Scripture, culminating in the atonement and Resurrection of Christ. In some circles, this kid [*sic*] of preaching avoids reference to Bible characters as moral examples and even avoids ethical applications of texts. In my opinion, the focus on redemptive history is often edifying though not biblically required. The avoidance of moral content

---

5. Ferguson, "Exegesis," 194–95.

> is, in my view, a distortion of biblical preaching, and such preaching is a distortion of Scripture.[6]

It is not difficult to see, then, that while redemptive-historical preaching has a place among the apolitical, it is superfluous to the priorities of preachers that are partisan.

- Topical preaching: a homiletical method focusing on issues or themes of current interest or concern. With its proof-texting approach to Scripture, topical preaching lends itself to the apolitical and party-political approaches.[7] Whereas the former put the proof-texting to an exclusive spiritual use, the latter employ it for partisan purposes. The biblical-political may use the approach on rare occasions—for example in national emergencies—but even then they seek to deal with the topic at hand in as exegetical and expository a manner as possible.

While all these styles of preaching contain worthy elements, I put it to you that none combines better a high estimate and reverent use of the Word on the one hand with the effective engagement of the culture war on the other, than expository preaching.

In the first place, expository preaching is the most comprehensive style available. It does greatest justice to the entirety of Scripture (the revealed counsel of God [Acts 20:27]), and expresses best Paul's maxim that "All Scripture is . . . profitable" (2 Tim 3:16). While it can be redemptive-historical (depending on the genre), contain doctrine, topics, and anecdotes, these other

---

6. Glossary, forthcoming *Festschrift* for John Frame, edited by John Hughes (Philipsburg, New Jersey: P&R, 2009).

7. Writes J. I. Packer, "In a topical sermon the text is reduced to a peg on which the speaker hangs his line of thought; the shape and thrust of the message reflect his own best notions of what is good for people rather than being determined by the text itself" ("Introduction: Why Preach?" 4).

methods of preaching are not necessarily expository, certainly not in a consecutive sense, and do not guarantee the utilization of the breadth of Scripture covered in ongoing systematic exposition.

Secondly, systematic exposition is the best method of preaching available for expressing the biblical worldview and its application to every sphere of life, the political included. While the method does not require the sequential exposition of Scripture from Genesis through Revelation, its use of both Testaments and all genres of Scripture guarantees the coverage of biblical territory left uncovered by a random approach to the choice of passage or text. Writes John Stott, "the thorough and systematic opening up of a large portion of Scripture broadens people's horizons [and] introduces them to some of the Bible's major themes, and shows them how to interpret Scripture by Scripture."[8]

Thirdly, the very discipline of systematic exposition bridles the minister's personal predilections. Experience reveals that ministers whose practice is to preach an array of randomly chosen texts—as is common in the anecdotal and topical approaches especially—inevitably lean toward their own interests and hobbyhorses, or toward those texts easiest to unpack. The hobbyhorse may vary from minister to minister, but it is not difficult to imagine how tempting it is for preachers with large political appetites to transform their pulpits into political soapboxes.[9] Preachers resist this temptation by self-regulation—better put, by biblical regulation—critical to which is the acceptance of the primacy of the Word, the necessity of its in-depth study, and an attitude of submission to its teaching.

8. Stott, *I Believe in Preaching*, 316.

9. It is uncertain whether Bopp's advice that, "a pastor may individually and personally endorse candidates for political office" ("Do's and Don'ts for Political Activities for Pastors"), includes his pulpit deliverances. It is clear, however, that if he does so he must underline the fact that he is airing a personal opinion. In reality, however, party-political preachers subtly or not so subtly make their allegiances known without actually mentioning the name of the party.

Fourthly, systematic exposition broadens the range of application. Motivated by dedication to the applied exposition of the Word and reliant on the illumination of the Holy Spirit, the genuine expositor follows the principles of the text to the array of applications it suggests to his active mind and humble heart. He understands and accepts that application is only biblical when it correlates with what is in the book or passage under review, surveyed by means of sound exegesis and reliable hermeneutics.[10] Whether then it is the Scripture that brings us to the application (the norm) or the current event that brings us to the Scripture (the exception), the details of the application must be rooted in the scripture under review. When it is, the preacher can engage the culture war effectively without betraying his calling.

3. THE MAXIMIZATION OF THE BIBLICAL WORLDVIEW

Paul G. Hieberts defines "worldview" as the "fundamental cognitive, affective, and evaluative presuppositions a group of people make about the nature of things, which they use to order their lives."[11] Put more simply, "Worldviews are what people in a com-

10. Writes Bernard Ramm,
  . . . the message from the pulpit will be Biblical, exegetical, and expository. Holy Scripture is the source and norm of preaching; exegesis is the scientific ascertaining of the meaning of the text; and exposition is its relevant proclamation to the congregation. The concept which binds these three together is the concept of the Word of God. The Scripture is the Word of God understood; and preaching is the Word of God made relevant to time and place. This high view of preaching as an important form of the Word of God is in keeping with the high view of preaching maintained at the time of the Reformation by both Luther and Calvin (*Hermeneutics*, 9–10).

11. Hiebert, *Transforming Worldviews*, 15. Hiebert notes the problems

munity take as given realities, the maps they have of reality that they use for living." Briefer still, they are parts of culture serving as the substructure on which cultures are built.[12] In a biblical or Christian worldview, the major realities include God (his existence, attributes, work, and sovereignty over all), man (his privileges, finitude, dependence, fallenness, and accountability), the gospel (its focus on Christ's person and work and his impact on individual, communal and cosmic redemption). With the breakdown of the widespread homogeneity of Judeo-Christian worldview in Western society, Christians have had to realize the need of going public with the biblical worldview that was once assumed. We do so in obedience to the commission of Christ (Matt 28:18–20)—a commission that includes within the making of disciples the dissemination of the biblical worldview.

The biblical-political approach enables preachers to expound and to utilize this worldview effectively; that is, from an informed understanding of its relevance to the present. In the background here is Francis Schaeffer's belief that twentieth-century cultural changes were understood by the church in bits and pieces rather than in total.[13] We failed to see decisions over permissiveness, pornography, the public schools, the breakdown of the family, and abortion as part—a symptom if you like—of a shift in worldview from something "at least vaguely Christian" towards something more akin to impersonal chance. Schaeffer attributes this failure to "a defective view of Christianity"—a reference to what we have described here as the narrowness of the apolitical approach. This defective view, he explains,

> . . . has its roots in the Pietist movement under the leadership of P. J. Spener in the seventeenth century. Pietism

associated with the term "worldview," but defends its use until a better term is found on the grounds of its familiarity and functionality.

12. Hiebert, *Transforming Worldviews*, 80.

13. Schaeffer, *A Christian Manifesto* in *The Complete Works*, 5:423; *cf.* 493.

> began as a healthy protest against formalism and a too abstract Christianity. But it had a deficient "platonic" spirituality. It was platonic in the sense that Pietism made a sharp division between the "spiritual" and the "material" world—giving little, or no, importance to the "material" world. The totality of human existence was not afforded a proper place. In particular it neglected the intellectual dimension of Christianity.[14]

Regrettably, what Schaeffer calls the "poor side of Pietism and its resulting platonic outlook" lingers among many present-day, self-perceived Puritans. The apolitical approach is an evidence of this, and contributes in part to the reactionary catch-up efforts of the party-political.

Rejecting the hyper-spiritualization of apolitical ministry, preachers of a biblical-political bent also refuse the carnality of the party-political overreaction. Insisting that the Bible is not a handbook of political philosophy, they nevertheless understand that the exposition of Scripture brings into view through the gospel a true political philosophy or biblical worldview.[15] Ed Dobson typifies this understanding well. Exchanging his high-profile work for the Moral Majority for a return to pastoral ministry, he decided to avoid all political entanglements in order to focus on the Bible:

> I would not get off on tangents but would consistently teach the Bible verse by verse. Over the years I have tried to do this. In teaching the Bible one cannot avoid the

---

14. Schaeffer, *A Christian Manifesto* in *The Complete Works*, 5:424; *cf.* 451.

15. To quote Maritain:
> If it is correct to say that there will always be rightist temperaments and leftist temperaments, it is nevertheless also correct to say that political philosophy is neither rightist nor leftist; it must simply be true (*The Twilight of Civilization*, 41).

moral issues of our day.... Keeping the pulpit free of
politics does not mean keeping it free of clear, biblical,
moral teaching.[16]

Critical to the Bible's true political philosophy or worldview is the wisdom Scripture teaches.[17] Although much of this wisdom dates back to the Pentateuch, and to the days of Israel's theocracy, its principles may be expounded without employing what Budziszewski calls "inflationary strategies."[18] Indeed, many

---

16. Thomas and Dobson, *Blinded by Might*, 158. Dobson kept his word as a pastor, but as I go to print upset has broken out in Grand Rapids over his revelation in the press that he voted for Barack Obama. The upset is due not only to the vote itself (the evident contradiction between Obama's view of abortion and the stance of the Moral Majority), but to Dobson's termination of his silence about politics. While not in a position to comment with any authority on the issue, it seems to me, with regard to the latter issue, that Dobson's retirement from pastoral ministry does afford him greater liberty to speak about politics, although the possession of this liberty does mean to say that it is always wise to exercise it.

17. Lord Blanch of Bishopthorpe writes: "I believe that the Scriptures provide a valuable source of argument, reflection and aspiration which is not irrelevant to the issues which dominate and disturb Western society. We must not be deterred by the distance in time and space of these ancient writings. Whatever our private attitudes to them may be, they are the product of the Judeo-Christian tradition which has been hugely influential in the forming of our public institutions, our educational practice, our underlying attitudes to life. Secular, pluralistic, we may be, but we remain inheritors of a tradition which took its rise in the Sinai desert some three thousand years ago. In that sense we cannot undo the past and we would be wise not to ignore it" ("Is There any Word from the Lord?" 81).

18. He mentions three strategies in particular. The assumption that (1) God's code for ancient Israel reflects the divine blueprint for all civil law; (2) the biblical pattern of covenant represents the divine blueprint for all political authority; (3) the policies adopted by biblical rulers reflect God's blueprint for governmental policy in general (*Evangelicals in the Public Square*, 27ff.).

of these principles have been carried over by Christ into the New Testament era, for application in these last days. They shape not only our thinking but our living, albeit in ways appropriate to the new covenant maturity of the church.[19] These principles are individual, domestic, ecclesial, and social in character.

Those principles *individually* applicable focus on God's call to repentance and faith, and to the new life of structured freedom promised in Christ to those who heed it. The new lives Christians possess enable them to serve as salt and light in society. The history of Western society illustrates this full well.[20] Explains Colson: "Christianity is the only religious system that provides for *both* individual concerns and the ordering of a society with liberty and justice for all."[21] He continues: "The Kingdom of God provides unique moral imperatives that can cause men and women to rise above their natural egoism to serve the greater good. God intends His people to do this; furthermore, He commands them to influence the world through their obedience to Him, not by taking over the world."[22] The present state of Western Europe gives us some idea of how costly is the loss of this God consciousness; although, in fairness, the spiritual deterioration of many of the European Union countries may be due to varied factors, among the most notable being the unbiblical liberalism, privatization, separatism, and hyper-spiritualization of Christian witness.[23]

Those principles *domestically* applicable relate to ethical responsibilities pertaining to household, sexual, and work relations. In the pluralistic day in which we live, it is very possible for

19. The crucial passage explaining the maturing of the church is Galatians 3:23—4:7.

20. D'Souza, *What's So Great About Christianity?* 77.

21. Colson, *God & Government*, 267.

22. Ibid., 268.

23. The influx of Eastern European countries into the European Union may challenge this deterioration, given the failure of the Communist suppression of Christian belief in the Soviet bloc.

Christians to buy into the popular notion of "each to their own," and to regard lifestyle diversities in these areas as acceptable, even good. After all, are we not told that polarization — the "mission . . . to divide . . . along political and cultural lines"[24]—entails the movement within a democracy by a minority to affect adversely the majority?[25] Yes, but think about this. For all the present activity of secular progressives, can it be said with any seriousness that the Judeo-Christian perspective on domestic ethical responsibilities is a minority viewpoint, let alone one with adverse affects? Great play may be made of abuses, but all these prove is the fallenness of human nature. They neither demonstrate the datedness or falsity of Judeo-Christian ethics, nor the need of putting Western society through an entire experiment in secular-progressive diversity to learn the costs of spurning our personal responsibilities!

We are therefore to uphold marriage—one man with one woman for life—countering moves that would promote serial marriage, open marriage, polygamy, and homosexual aberrations. We do so, not as a power play aimed at holding onto the religious hegemony of the nation, but as a means of sustaining the institution God established at creation for the benefit of all in society. While we have a special pastoral care for those in the church, and therefore fight for those oppressed by greed and corruption (Jas 5:1–6), our proclamation of the gospel to all is intended not only to save the lost but to challenge the epicenters of injustice. We take up this fight not with carnal weapons, but "by doing good unto all men" (Gal 6:10). We therefore promote among other things a good work ethic and a benevolent management style (Col 4:1). We express practical concern for the unacceptable inequality of wealth among nations, for we share the resources of the same earth as one human race. We refuse to use the promise of a new earth to ravage unthinkingly the resources of the present planet (Rom 8:18–23).

24. Thomas and Beckel, *Common Ground*, 40.
25. Ibid., 41, 45.

Then there are those *ecclesial* principles relevant to the worship, witness, and service of the Christian family. This is the realm of evangelism and apologetics relevant to the defense of the gospel *vis à vis* competing views of God and the world. These issues are so much the bread and butter issues of pulpit ministry and church life that I just mention them here in passing.

Finally, there are the *social* principles; those most likely to get overlooked by apolitical preachers. As present-day leadership guru John C. Maxwell rightly explains: "One of our problems is that ethics is never a business issue or a social issue or a political issue. It is always a personal issue."[26] Stott reminds us likewise by reference to the fourth beatitude: "Blessed are those who hunger and thirst for righteousness for they shall be satisfied" (Matt 5:6). The righteousness Jesus had in view, Stott teaches, was not simply legal (our right standing [justification] before God) or moral (the Christian's obligation to be upright), but social.

Social righteousness reflects God's attributes of justice and mercy and his concern for redemption, order, and fairness among his image bearers. It speaks of man's liberation from oppression, and addresses specific questions of slavery, poverty and hunger, violence, crime, racism, and nationalism. It promotes civil rights, justice, and integrity.[27] Indicting the evils of the church and the world (1 Pet 4:17), scriptural principles of social righteousness also teach non-retaliation on the one hand, and if that is not a

26. Maxwell, *Ethics 101*, 9.

27. Stott, *The Message of the Sermon on the Mount*, 45.

Presently the gay community, in fighting for gay marriage, is keen to equate gay rights with civil rights. Orthodox Christians resist this equation. For whereas civil rights speak of matters settled by creation, gay rights speak of matters denied by creation. That said, what is clear to orthodox Christians from a spiritual angle is less clear in the political context. While we reject the notion of gay marriage, our protests must comport with our understanding of church-state relations. In this and many other regards, advocates of the Establishment Principle can go further than their Voluntaryist counterparts, although without guarantee of success.

tall enough order, the proactive love of our enemies on the other (Matt 5:38–48; Lk 6:27–6). So does Paul (Rom 12:14–13:5). All in all, biblical references to social righteousness point the way to the achievement of order amid the messiness of our fallen world. They do so in a context in which God has promised redemption that is not only personal to the believer, but also cosmic (Matt 19:28; Rom 8:18–25).

In preaching social righteousness, the biblical-political preacher indicates the broader utilitarian appeal of his ministry. For the expounding of the Bible's lessons in social righteousness breaks down the compartmentalization of the sacred and the secular. All the same, the biblical-political preacher does not force the exposition of social righteousness. Rather, he allows Scripture to determine the addressing of such issues, specifically the "When?" and the "How?" By doing so, he relinquishes the fear of being deemed left-wing. What matters to him is the exposition of the whole revealed counsel of God and the addressing of the needs of those divine image-bearers dehumanized by structures of injustice.

While it takes both a well-defined biblical world-and-life view and maturing expository skills to preach fully these individual, domestic, ecclesial, and social principles of Scripture, many of us need in addition to engage the culture war better than we do. Apolitical preachers could do with proclaiming more of the scope of Scripture, its theology, and application. They could also do a better job of balancing heavenly mindedness and earthly usefulness. By the same token, party-political preachers need to be more cautious than they have been in claiming biblical support for issues that Scripture leaves open or unaddressed. It is especially important that we eschew the political classification of our pulpit deliverances, notwithstanding the current secularization of the Democratic Party.[28] What should matter most

28. It is unclear to what degree the more centrist Democrat winners of the 2006 elections have exercised a restraining influence on the party's secularist drift. It appears that talk of God has increased, but many a

to us is that our hearers think biblically—that is, *supra* or *trans* party-politically—even if the voting booth demands we become party-political in the moment of casting our vote.

Our chief role is to help our congregants think "Christianly," so that they decide political matters freely and yet thinkingly. Where congregations are blessed with such maturity—the ability to think and act "Christianly"—they will neither need nor want their minister(s) to tell them how to vote.[29] After all, the ballot is secret. The only circumstance in which we may legitimately direct our hearers in the use of their vote is in cases where it is universally clear to Bible-believing Christians that one or more parties are bent on breaking God's law (Acts 5:29).

To the party-political preacher, this biblical-political approach appears lame and possibly suspicious. In part we may sympathize with this, for, as we have acknowledged, undoubtedly there is room for development of the nexus between proclamation and apologetics in the sociocultural arena, notably in the pursuit of social righteousness. But if the truth be known, the party-political preacher's real complaint may well be that the Scriptures do not back clearly enough the party of his choice. The message of Scripture has political ramifications, and these the biblical-political preacher seeks to follow through on; but Scripture stops so very far short of serving as a political manifesto. Writes Budziszewski:

> The problem for evangelical political thinkers is not that the Bible contains no political teachings (for it does) but that the Bible does not provide enough *by itself* for an adequate political theory. Although important general

---

skeptical Christian voter rightly hesitates to deduce that talk of God equates to action self-consciously taken with a view to his pleasure.

29. This assumes our congregants decide to vote. For the various arguments against Christian participation in the electoral process see Lewis's *Electing Not to Vote*. It seems to me that contributors to the volume have proven the legitimacy of abstention, but not its necessity.

> principles about government can indeed be drawn from
> Scripture, the list of such principles is short.[30]

When we pass off our partisan opinion for the authority of the Word of God we may fool our hearers, some we may even please (assuming we interpret God's Word according to their own political preferences); but the reality is we betray our calling.[31] A loss of divine pleasure, biblical authority, and vocational satisfaction inevitably results.

4. THE ENSURING OF CERTAIN CRITICAL BIBLICAL EMPHASES

Three critical biblical emphases come to mind: the Lordship of Christ over the conscience, the sovereignty of God, and the preeminence of the Kingdom of Heaven. These we consider here in turn.

Clearly the biblical-political approach affords room for Christ's Lordship over the conscience. Those utilizing the approach may not be able to fathom why other Christians vote the way they do, but they realize that we have no authority to tell them

30. Budziszewski, *Evangelicals in the Public Square*, 23.

31. What divine authority do we preachers have, for instance, to proclaim whether God wishes Northern Ireland to be part of the U.K. or Eire, or, more generally, whether God is Republican or Democrat (U.S.), Tory, Labour or Liberal Democrat (U.K.)? We have none at all. Which explains why partisan or party-political preachers draw only tangentially from Scripture. Typically, they either introduce it at the outset, proceeding thereafter to deliver a message that has little relevance to the passage read, or they conclude with a text or passage distantly related at best to the content of the message. Either way, Scripture loses its foundational role under the party-political approach. It becomes but an add-on feature—a legitimization if you like—of the use of the pulpit for political rhetoric. Along the way, something is lost of the transcendence of the sermon (a word from God) amid the demands for relevance (the need we have of a word for man).

which way to vote, or to coerce them to vote the way we would. Our responsibility is to expound and to apply Scripture as fairly as we can (fully cognizant of our accountability to God), urging our congregants to fulfill their civic responsibilities in line with the dictates of their Christian consciences (see ch. 3). It is simply not acceptable, therefore, for preachers to say from their pulpits, as I heard one brother do, "The law of the land forbids me from telling you what to vote, but whatever you do, vote right!" Such a use of the pulpit is not only a probable violation of the law (at least in the U.S.), it is a breach of his privileged position; an exercise of oversight by compulsion, domineering those under our charge by the willful lording of their consciences (1 Pet 5:2–3). What Dietrich Bonhoeffer once said of Christians in general must be remembered by preachers in particular; namely, that "we are not lords, but instruments in the hand of the Lord of history."[32]

The liberty biblical-political preachers afford their congregants is not to be interpreted as an indifference to the serious issues of legitimate government and politics; nor as a lack of support for the promotion of Christian ideals in the nation. Rather, it is a humble acceptance of the fact that no matter how strongly I may believe in one political party or ideology over another, there are other Christians my equal in insight and faithfulness who think differently. This we find easier to accept when we appreciate that Christians often focus on different issues when deciding which way to vote.

Two Christians, for example, may value equally the sanctity of human life. But this cherished principle leads one of them to vote Republican in the hope of furthering the pro-life agenda and traditional family values, while the other votes Democrat in the belief the party will do better at countering inner-city poverty and supporting developing countries (an issue of the sanctity of life for families caught up in famine and disease). Both interpretations of the Christian principle are honorably intentioned, but one sibling

32. Bonhoeffer, *Letters & Papers from Prison*, 145.

within the family of God prioritizes the one set and their solutions, and the next the other. Regrettably, the democratic process, governed as it is by the party system, forces the voter to choose a package of policies, when she/he may prefer to mix and match those offered by opposing parties. Put simply, the ballot box does not allow great leeway for nuanced thinking. All thinking voters are left hoping that the politician of their choice acts on matters (of conscience especially) in a way pleasing to God.[33] Hope, however, is chiefly what we have once the politician's immediate accountability to the electorate has subsided.

Besides honoring Christ's Lordship over the conscience, the biblical-political approach also stresses trust in the sovereignty of God.[34] We teach our people that God remains enthroned regardless of the outcome of each successive election. No matter how often, how much, or how loudly a candidate may proclaim himself or herself to be the agent of change—in fact the change they've been waiting for, to borrow Obama's words—there is no utopia prior to the *eschaton*. By the same token, experience reminds us that, in democracies, those we fear gaining power are rarely as destructive as our fears envision them being.[35] The

---

33. In the U.K. parliament, at least, politicians have free votes on issues of conscience, but there are no guarantees they will use them the way we Christians would desire them to. Referenda are generally so infrequent as not to count for the present purposes.

34. This sovereignty constitutes a supremacy embracing the state as well as society and the church (Kuyper, *Lectures on Calvinism*, 79ff.).

35. Writes Lord Blanch: "It is unlikely that we shall wake up one fine morning and find the whole world Liberal, Socialist or Conservative. But we could wake up one morning and find the whole world transfigured with a strange radiance, and realize that the unthinkable has come to pass—God has entered his kingdom and reigns" ("Is There any Word from the Lord?" 98)

One exception to this may be the slowly corroding influence of successive New Labour governments on the Judeo-Christian principles and morals undergirding the British establishment. This influence was

adversarial character of party politics, which fosters so much polarization, is very often accompanied by scaremongering. Without encouraging indifference or naiveté, we may be thankful for the many checks and balances within democracies that preclude the abuse of power, the reality of which our Christian brothers and sisters experience in lands where dictatorships and rigged elections are the norm.

Yet biblical-political preachers focus on God's sovereignty not simply to comfort their hearers when the winds of political change suggest the likelihood of economic and moral decline, but to help them focus on the Kingdom of Heaven: the immediate expression of God's sovereignty on earth (his kingdominion). This Kingdom is to be ultimate in the affections and focus of God's people, taking precedence over our party-political preferences and national loyalties.[36] When we accord it the place it warrants, we understand very well that what matters ultimately is not the color of the party in power, or the standing of our country, but whether the Kingdom of Christ is progressing (Acts 1:3f.).[37] As James Skillen observes:

---

probably summed up best by the press secretary of Tony Blair, Alastair Campbell, who famously quipped "We don't do God." Tony Blair's post-premiership conversion to Roman Catholicism has been, in some ways, a going against the tide of his own party. Christian Republicans in America fear a similar corrosion under President Obama.

36. See Ed Dobson's comments in Thomas and Dobson, *Blinded by Might*, 48.

37. Many British Christians lament the fact that the U.K. is not the country it used to be. My father summed up this melancholy a number of years ago, when offering his stock reply to those asking what he wanted for his birthday: "I want my country back!" We all knew what he meant. The U.K.'s spiritual and moral decline has been pitiful to observe. Living in America is beginning to feel like *déjà vu*, with many Christians fearful the U.S. is going the same way as Western Europe. Adding to this apprehension is the concern that up-and-coming super powers such as China and India will fill the political vacuum created by God's rejection of an America intent on spurning her spiritual heritage.

> ... too many Christians continue to see America through civil-religious glasses as God's specially chosen nation [the same post-imperial tendency lingers in Great Britain]. They are willing to use both cross- and crown-language to describe the United States instead of confining the language to God's new nation: the multigenerational, worldwide church of Christ. Their civil-religious nationalism is what must be rejected by showing that God's new nation in Christ, the bride of Christ, will be satisfied with nothing less than the final revelation of God's Kingdom, which cannot be achieved by human political means.[38]

Paradoxically, it is by pursuing the counter-cultural agenda of Christ's Kingdom that we preachers perceive most the present dangers, and benefit most the kingdoms of this earth, not least our own. Sometimes the breadth and depth of the biblically based details of this biblical-political approach offend the right and sometimes the left, and sometimes both. Preaching faithfully the fullness of Christ's message of the Kingdom, we let the chips fall where they may. Applying the expounded Word in this way, our preaching becomes prophetic, its authority assured.

5. THE PROTECTION OF CONGREGATIONAL UNITY

There is little doubt that America's deep political divisions have impacted the unity of the country's congregations.[39] Combining an acceptance of the limits of involvement in the culture war

---

38. Skillen, "Where Kingdom Politics Should Lead Us," 85.

39. There are a number of reasons why American churches seem more greatly impacted than those that are British. Not only are Christians more numerous in the U.S. than in the U.K., they have thereby a more significant voice in the public square. Furthermore, the Democratic and Republican parties have stuck to their ideological roots more than appears to be the case with British political parties, notwithstanding the current secular progressive influences abroad in the U.S.

with an understanding of the importance of liberty of conscience, submission to God, and the priorities of the Kingdom of Heaven, biblical-political preachers are best placed to engage the issues of the day without dividing the church.

The apolitical preacher inadvertently threatens congregational unity by transforming it into a narrower concept of uniformity. Remaining largely silent about the humongous issues of the culture war and Scripture's relevance to them, he risks losing his relevance.[40] Congregants alert to the challenges awhirl in the realm of current affairs quickly become frustrated by their pastor's lopsided other-worldly focus. Where this situation persists, such congregants either drift off in search of a ministry that impacts them domestically and vocationally, or they remain to grin and bear the dissatisfaction of having an out-of-touch pastor. His apolitical ministry may continue to attract a band of other-worldly minded folk, who have gone A.W.O.L. from the culture war raging around them; nonetheless, such congregations become increasingly obscurantist, surreal, or ghetto-like (hiding away from the reality of the world's happenings, preferring to dream of the celestial world to come). They may know the issues, but speak of them only to condemn the "other side" from a safe distance. These denunciations may satisfy their consciences, but they do little to engage the battle or to witness *effectively* to those they deem enemies. Meanwhile, the ethically broken and morally dysfunctional of their community are left ignored or judged and stigmatized among the folk of the church, the imprisoned deserted, the unjust unchallenged, and the unborn and the dying unspoken for.

By contrast, party-political preachers threaten congregational unity by introducing into their flocks a measure of sectarianism or segregation. This division begins subtly, perhaps even unwittingly, when the bounds of Scripture and of calling are overstepped. This introduces a creeping discomfort into the

---

40. By the adjective "humongous" I refer to the critical significance, size, and impact of the issues.

congregational experience of those drawing different political deductions than the pastor from the principles of Scripture. If left unchecked, this partisanship ends up isolating certain congregants from the "in crowd." Sensitive to what becomes in effect their second-class membership, brought about by their alertness to the distinction between the authority of God's Word and the preacher's personal political opinions, the offended gradually withdraw before their patience with the pastor's ascriptural declarations runs out.[41]

In moving on to sit under ministries of a more satisfactory character, the churches they leave behind come to reflect more and more but one sector of the electorate. The benefit of the unified congregation that remains is more than offset by the cost of those shut out of it. The more politically homogeneous the congregation becomes, the easier it is for the minister to become blatant in his partisanship. In the end, even a contrary bumper sticker or two in the parking lot becomes problematic to the minister and to those he influences most. Further isolation, even alienation, is experienced by those independent thinkers who stick it out at the church. They may be made to feel that there is something wrong with them, not least for failing to weigh the issues as "Christianly" as they ought.[42] Yet, it is the pastor who in an instance like this has gone awry. He has crossed that all-important line distinguishing the exposition of the Word from political indoctrination, and has thereby denied his flock their Christian liberty. In the words of Maritain, the Spirit who authored the Word and energizes those who preach it "is not a

41. Their disagreement may be theological (disagreement with the use of the pulpit for political pronouncements) and/or political (disagreement with the chosen position of the minister). In the worst-case scenarios, members rightly object to a minister appealing to them along political lines as a means of distraction from the paucity of his ecclesial leadership and pastoral care.

42. That is to say, within a Christian frame of reference (Stott, *I Believe in Preaching*, 170).

spirit of Empire or of party, of nation or of race, of clan or of faction."[43] Scripture does not grant support *in toto* to particular political packages, party programs, or manifestos. It is not for preachers to pretend it does.

This is a bitter pill for many Christians to swallow in the current climate, not least for those who climb the church's pulpits. Yet the biblical-political preacher is prepared to swallow, knowing that the pill serves the overall health of the church, not least its internal unity. Still, self-sacrifice and courage are required to apply the Scriptures consistently, sometimes praising and sometimes indicting the party of our own choice, and sometimes pleasing or displeasing those political animals peppered among our hearers. Yet, if we maintain a consistent approach to the exposition and application of Scripture, our hearers will come to appreciate in time that what matters most to us is loyalty to Christ. They will know that when the occasion arises naturally in applying the text of Scripture to praise or to critique government or opposition policy, our motivation is not partisan point-scoring but faithfulness to God. He it is who has called us to be objective heralds of his Word, exhibiting neither fear nor favor. This objectivity requires that we preach and exemplify the fact that in Christ "there is neither Jew nor Greek, . . . slave nor free, . . . male nor female . . ." (Gal 3:28). Nor is there is Republican or Democrat, Tory, Socialist, or Liberal Democrat. Our identity must be found in Christ no less today than in that of the apostle Paul (A.D.?–65?).

6. THE IMPROVEMENT OF CHRISTIAN WITNESS

The Christian church in the West has lived off the blessings of the past for too long. Indeed, we have been slow to realize the urgent need of *effective* evangelism notwithstanding the obvious

---

43. Maritain, *The Twilight of Civilization*, 31.

dwindling of so many congregations.⁴⁴ In our complacency we have assumed against the evidence that the folk will come back to the church at some point. Accordingly, many of our conservative churches have failed to engage the communities around their buildings, but think that because they have given out some tracts or held some open-air meetings their responsibilities are fulfilled. Having begun my ministry in this way, I believe firmly and sympathetically that there is a place for this sort of witness. In Britain at least, such methods stand as a testimony against a society in willful rebellion against God. They are, to use Paul's words, "a fragrance from death to death" (2 Cor 2:16). Nevertheless, it appears that God is using "as a fragrance from life to life" those endeavors that understand the varied approaches to evangelism in the New Testament and which set the proclamation of the Word in the context of friendship and relationship.⁴⁵

It would be well for the church to rethink the profile she accords evangelism and the effectiveness with which she undertakes it. Included in this rethink ought to be a consideration of how the church's political discourse (or otherwise) impacts her testimony.

History may well conclude that there has occurred among many British Evangelicals over the twentieth century a narrowing of the application of the gospel, with a resultant curtailing of the number of common social and political discussion points between the church and the world pertaining to the events and

44. I am thinking especially of the U.K., although concerns are being aired about the present statistics relating to congregational development in the U.S.

45. By the varied approaches I think chiefly of the distinction between the evangelism of those who had the (Hebrew) Scriptures and those who did not (*cf.* Acts 13:13–43 [esp. vv. 15 and 33] and 17:16–34 [esp. vv. 22–23]). *Christianity Explored*, emanating from All Souls' Church, Langham Place, London, under the leadership of Rico Tice, is being well used to mediate the Word evangelistically in a context of friendship and relationship. Many who have used the course can testify to both its faithfulness and effectiveness.

ideas of the day. Sensing the need of a widespread awakening whole generations of believers seem, with few exceptions, to have adopted a "let's await revival" solution that emphasizes the sovereignty of God at the expense of human responsibility. Defending this posture, the apolitical have rightly argued that legislation cannot change the human heart. What they ignore, however, is the role law has in challenging the heart's evil expression and in hindering the secular-progressive erosion of Judeo-Christian values from society. "Surely," writes Budziszewski, "it would be naïve to think that better laws eliminate the need for God's grace. But it is equally unrealistic to suppose that conversion cancels out the need for better laws."[46]

The hyper-spirituality of the apolitical approach to Christian witness may explain, in part at least, the rarity of unchurched visitors to conservative churches in my native Wales, and the small number of their conversions to Christ. Doubtless the gospel is going forth, but how often does it connect with the everyday concerns of the masses outside the church? In asking this, I am not appealing for some up-to-date equivalent of the social gospel, but I am observing how so few churches seem to connect socially in their evangelistic efforts. Pre-evangelism efforts aimed at meeting folk "where they are at" would help in building atmospheres conducive to the spread of the Word. It is here that the construction or recognition of common points between the church and the world, reminiscent of Paul's approach at Athens, are very helpful. These may even have a sociopolitical theme, when dealt with in a nonpartisan fashion, and when aimed at sharing in the first place the biblical worldview.

Rejecting the hyper-spiritualism or practical form of hyper-Calvinism (with its lopsided emphasis on God's sovereignty), the biblical-political approach stresses the ongoing ordinary influence of the Spirit by whose enabling we pursue social righteousness. While not ignoring the need for ecclesial revival

---

46. Budziszewski, *Evangelicals in the Public Square*, 47.

and societal awakening—for spiritual awakenings can further, exponentially so, the redemption of society and bring glory to God[47]—skillful advocates of the biblical-political approach are able to expound Scripture in such a way as to inform and challenge their hearers with the sorts of principles necessary to help them face weekly, via media saturation, the moment by moment bombardment of political happenings and issues. Biblical-political preachers urge, then, the socio-cultural-political engagement of our hearers while waiting, with them, on the Lord for the reviving of his church and the awakening of society. Of course, obedient engagement with the surrounding culture cannot guarantee revival nor awakening—for God is sovereign in opening the heavens—nevertheless, in his grace the Lord regularly honors and blesses his people for their obedience. Accordingly, we pursue the defense of certain laws and the pursuit of others as a means of preserving the Judeo-Christian basis of Western society; for it is in this context that we can best secure a rightful freedom to preach the gospel. After all, it is gospel preaching that has always been critical to a genuine spiritual awakening.

Apolitical preachers are not alone in impeding effective evangelism. Party-political preachers do, too. Rightly strong in expressing the urgency of the situation we face today, they nevertheless tend to blur the clarity of the church's presentation of Christ. The most common way this is done is by implying that conversion requires the transition from one party affiliation to another. Not only is this a precarious assumption, it can be manipulative. Writes Dobson:

> We need to make careful use of power and influence. People expect politicians to talk about politics, but when preachers start talking about politics, they begin using

---

47. D'Souza notes the impact of the First and Second Great Awakenings on the American Revolution and the Temperance Movement, the Movement for women's suffrage, and the abolitionist movement, respectively (*What's So Great About Christianity?* 72–73).

the power of their position to legitimize political issues. Preachers are perceived as spiritual leaders and authorities by the general public. When they defend political or social issues, they are perceived as somehow speaking for God. It is difficult for the average lay person to distinguish between whether the preacher is speaking for himself or God....[48]

By restricting formal political comment to issues of scriptural principle and application, biblical-political preachers ensure that Christ is the only offense of the gospel. The newly saved may change their political affiliation once converted, but the biblical-political preacher in seeking to be all things to all men that he may win some (1 Cor 9:19), is satisfied to let God work out those details after their conversion. For a new heart, replete with the submission it brings to God's Word and an openness to the principles of Scripture, changes significantly the scenario. We need, therefore, neither assume nor manipulate changes in political affiliation.[49] The chief lesson of the apostolic era is pertinent in this regard; namely, that Christ is received through faith alone. Two thousand years later the purity and (trans-cultural) simplicity of the gospel is no less important. The lost are no more obliged to alter their political affiliations in coming to Christ than the Gentiles of the first century were obliged to become Jews.

It is a serious business for preachers to play politics with the gospel. This error of judgment is compounded when we seek, however subtly, to align our congregations politically. The orchestrated political homogenization of congregational life cannot but be costly to the missional effectiveness of the church. What is more, it is irresponsible for partisan preachers to put

---

48. Thomas and Dobson, *Blinded by Might*, 49.

49. Naturally there are occasions when a change of political affiliation will serve as a sign of genuine conversion; such as in cases where the convert has previously supported a party or ideology undoubtedly in conflict with Christianity.

all their hopes for the redemption of society in the enacting of laws, even in those that are consistent with Scripture.⁵⁰ For all that laws can demonstrate in the final analysis is why members of society stand in need of Christ and his atonement. For when human legislation mirrors God's law and vindicates his justice (Rom 4:15), defines sin (Rom 4:15; 5:13), and arouses our rebellion (Rom 5:20),⁵¹ it can also teach us that atonement and forgiveness are only to be found in Christ. For this reason we preachers look beyond legislative appeal to the opportunities we have to press home the message of the gospel.

That said, the passing of laws has greater ramifications than the apolitical may appreciate, nonetheless only the gospel has the sort of dynamism needed to effect social change. By its truth, personified in Christ, the gospel changes the world from the inside out.⁵² Having a further and longer-lasting reach, we prefer the gospel's power to that offered by ideologies or party machinery (Rom 1:16), and resist the visible lure of the political process that tempts us to walk by sight rather than by faith.

What helps us retain our spiritual equilibrium is the clear teaching of Scripture. We recall that our weapons are spiritual (*cf.* 2 Cor 10:4), our Commander-in-Chief invisible (for the present [Acts 1:11]), and our mission heavenly. Confident of our Commander, our weapons, and our mission, we aim beyond the moralization of society, toward its salvation. Were we to aim at less (the former), we would no doubt moralize some, perhaps even many, but would see few if any saved. If, by contrast, we aim at the latter (the salvation of society), we shall by God's grace see some

---

50. Ed Dobson describes this way of thinking as "one of the dangers of mixing politics and religion" (*Blinded by Might*, 69).

51. This it does to procure the conviction that turns us to Christ.

52. Critiquing the party-political, Thomas and Dobson write: "If the Religious Right focuses mainly on politics to deliver us, we will never get that right because politics and government cannot reach into the soul. That is something God reserves for himself" (*Blinded by Might*, 13).

saved, perhaps even many, and many moralized besides.[53] Hence we put God's priorities first. We do so not only because this is the path of obedience, but because it is tactically astute to do so.

7. THE UPHOLDING OF CHRISTIAN ETHICS

The biblical-political approach challenges the bitterness that has crept from the political arena into the church. Each evening American Christians wishing to catch the news on television are forced to make a political choice.[54] It seems that whichever channel we opt for, partisanship is evident at least to some degree, as is evident from the accusations that competing channels are partial. Each channel, I dare say, could claim Fox News Channel's slogan "We report, you decide." The reality is, however, that the diet of political jousting ranges from juvenile point scoring—stressful screeching even, little different from the neighbors upstairs—to the outright massaging of statistics and arguments.

It is regrettable that Fox News Channel, such a friend to Christianity on the one hand, is not averse to these traits. I say regrettable because the church, explicitly her apolitical sectors, could learn much from the passion with which the network is fighting back against the determined secular-progressive assault on the Judeo-Christian values of the West.[55] The enjoyment of the channel is tempered, however, by those ugly traits of conservatism that some of Fox's faces exhibit. These traits may spike the ratings and shoot their books up the best-seller lists (a matter of which Bill O'Reilly commonly boasts), but, in my view, they don't always enhance the case for Judeo-Christian values and are

---

53. I draw this point from the maxim of nineteenth-century Scottish churchman and social reformer Thomas Chalmers (1780–1847): "For every ten the gospel saves, it moralizes fifty."

54. The same could be said of many British newspapers.

55. One example is the *O'Reilly Factor*'s 2008 "We say Merry Christmas" sticker campaign.

highly unlikely to render sympathetic, far less win over, many secular progressives ("the pinheads").

Maybe there is a cultural reaction in my assessment, but am I alone among Fox's sympathetic viewers in finding Sean Hannity's conservatism loaded, nauseating, pompous, and sometimes superficial?[56] Or John Gibson's jingoism obnoxious; the otherwise likable O'Reilly bullying, egotistical, and belittling;[57] and the time allowed the brash and sometimes callous Ann Coulter unwarranted?[58] These traits may be excused in part by the

---

56. Thomas and Beckel describe Hannity as a leading right-wing polarizer in the world of broadcasting, comparable to Al Franken on the left (*Common Ground*, 6). In fairness to Hannity, Beckel describes him as a prince off television although a pain on it (ibid. 264). While repetition is typically an effective means of teaching, in Hannity's case it seems to have become the substitute for substantive and objective reasoning. I cannot help but think that Hannity receives less of a hearing than he would otherwise.

57. Challenging O'Reilly's belief that his popularity is due to his "common sense" approach to politics and culture, the satirist Michael Savage writes: "No, Porky, I think people watch your show for the same reason they go to NASCAR races—to see the wrecks" (*The Political Zoo*, 237). Savage is likely correct here. Watch O'Reilly and it is not difficult to see how he operates. Those regarding it as futile to face him in interview are harangued until they bow to public pressure; but once they take up the challenge to come on the *O'Reilly Factor* they find themselves shouted down and unable to share their viewpoint without interruption. The Barney Frank interview of October 2, 2008, is a case in point. Built up by O'Reilly as a disreputable monster, Frank was afforded no opportunity to condemn himself by his own mouth. The interview may have spiked the ratings, but did little if anything to help viewers see clearly the truth.

58. Ann Coulter is described with some justification by Thomas and Beckel as a polarizer of the bottom-feeder variety comparable to Michael Moore on the left. Bottom-feeders are "polarizers who make money by keeping politics inflamed in order to sell books, maintain readership, sustain ratings, fill speaking schedules, or sell tickets" (*Common Ground*, 6). Allowing for the reality and legitimacy of righteous anger, it is nevertheless worth asking how Coulter, a professing Christian, can

pressures of the culture war, but the winsome presence of others on the network like Fox's Allstars, notably the Beltway Boys (Mort Kondracke and Fred Barnes, and various substitute "boys" [e.g., Juan Williams]), demonstrates the fact that the conservative case does not have to be counterproductive nor cross-party discussion acrimonious. The fact that some of the primetime programs are, is a reminder that although there are strong points of contact between the Judeo-Christian outlook of the church and Fox News Channel, the church ought not to take the standard of its dialogue from Fox news. The church is in the business of truth alone; the media mixes it with ratings-driven entertainment.

In the Christian apologetic there is a place for righteous anger. Its motivation, however, is the glory of God and the honor of Jesus Christ. It is typically aimed at leaders in disbelief and unspiritual revolt, and keeps in view the example of Christ who was as full of grace as he was of truth (John 1:14). Grace affords little opportunity for boasting or for bullying. It does ensure, however, that the opposition to Judeo-Christian values is governed by the values themselves and not by the attitudes with which they are espoused. Says the Proverb, "A soft anger turns away wrath, But a harsh word stirs up anger. The tongue of the wise uses knowledge rightly, But the mouth of fools pours forth foolishness" (Prov 15:1). "Unafraid," Fox analysts may be, but the claim of being "fair and balanced" is misleading. At face value it implies the channel is nonpartisan, when evidently many of the personnel go beyond offering a corrective to the left-wing media. We understand the claim more accurately when we hear Fox to

---

function this way with a seemingly clear conscience and no hesitation. How does her book *How to Speak to a Liberal (If You Must): The World According to Ann Coulter* comport with the importance and tenor of Christian witness? Her attitude may sell books; alas it also sells down the river biblical principles of witness and does little it seems to improve the ethics of politics.

offer fairness and balance *from an overall pro-right wing stance.*⁵⁹ What seems like the less than full disclosure of this matter makes Fox look, in this regard, like just another channel: loaded politically and obsessed by ratings.

It is precisely because the issues at stake are so important, that we need in the church and in society discussion that is genuinely open, honest, and truly balanced.⁶⁰ Presently, the unadorned facts are hard to come by. A blatant partisanship feeds the postmodern mindset that questions whether anything heard is true. Even when a news channel puts together pundits of divergent political views—as on *Crossfire* (CNN) or *Hannity and Colmes* (Fox)—the quality of discussion is poor.⁶¹ Truth and accuracy suffer at the hands of the adversarial approach so critical to entertainment and the sustenance of the ratings. Where entertainment (cheap point-scoring) triumphs over substance, balanced argumentation falls prey to raucous shouting matches. The United Kingdom is in a pitiful spiritual and moral state — as is reflected by the low morals and political correctness of na-

---

59. Writes Savage, "If Hannity is the favorite son of the RNC, the one who makes mommy and daddy proud by dressing smartly and never saying a bad word about the family, O'Reilly is his cantankerous older brother. He may throw a barb or two about mom's meatloaf to prove his edgy independence, but he still lives in his parents' basement" (*The Political Zoo*, 238). The tone of the trailers for *Glenn Beck* suggested the new program could serve as a counter to what seems to be the more blatantly partisan commentary of some on the Network. It is too early yet to say whether the program differs, say, from *Hannity* or other programs with their varying strengths and weaknesses.

60. While the tone of Savage's satire is very much part of the current climate, his depiction of members of the political zoo makes a most refreshing change from the loaded discussions the news channels daily feed us.

61. "Polarization was the model presented for many years on CNN's *Crossfire*. It was an appropriate name for a show. The problem with cross fire is that people in the middle tend to get shot" (Thomas and Beckel, *Common Ground*, 36).

tional television — but the *political* independence of the BBC and ITV does at least free the news from the partisan madness of American coverage. British viewers only have to compare the relative calmness of the news coverage on national television to the raucous nature of Prime Minister's Question Time in the House of Commons to see the difference.[62]

My point in all this is to wonder how much the church is affected by the acrimonious spirit daily invading our homes through the news media (Phil 4:8). If the apolitical preacher seeks to get away from it all by preferring blissful isolation, the party-political preacher is in danger of encouraging his congregation to ape the bitterness seen each evening on television. Whereas the former is seriously lacking in righteous anger, and embarrassed by or thoughtless about the outspokenness of Christ we read of in the New Testament, the latter expresses anger in ways that quickly become carnal if left unchecked.

Occupying the middle ground, the biblical-political preacher rejects the irrelevance of the apolitical while resisting the ethical challenges of the partisan. He expresses anger, but seeks God for the grace to ensure that it is righteous. Ideally, his passion is motivated by the Holy Spirit, focused on the concerns that matter most to God, expressed within the limits set by Scripture, bathed in prayer, and directed not so much against the foot soldiers of the secularist revolution (the "ordinary Joes"), but against the "generals" who oversee the de-Christianizing of society (the occupants of power, whether political [members of the Executive, Legislative, and Judiciary] or cultural [the Hollywood elite]). Enlisting under Christ's banner, the biblical-political preacher understands that it matters not only what battles we choose, but how we fight, and what forces we engage.

---

62. We can be thankful for the sake of the British democracy that the second chamber—the House of Lords—possesses sufficient occupancy of experts to debate the issues at a higher level.

The biblical-political preacher draws on the power of God and the sharpness of his Word to negate the movers and shakers of the day. By the same token, he appeals for fairness and balance in the Christian's waging of the culture war. This likely entails the countering of the blanket assumptions that Democrats who are "pro-choice" are necessarily "pro-Abortion." In the present polarized climate they may be lumped in with the morally indifferent when in fact they are simply wanting to ensure that in a crisis the mother's life receives priority, or, that under a scenario in which the laws are tightened, there is not a boom in back-street abortions. It seems to me then, that to hastily and perhaps willfully describe those labeled "pro-choice" as "pro-abortion" is to engage in the politics of polarization. I do not wish to be naïve about the horrors of abortion (for I am not), nor to pretend that the issues of weaponry are as straightforward, but how would those "pro-guns" appreciate being automatically labeled "pro-violence"? Likewise the biblical-political preacher counters blanket assumptions that Republicans are oil grabbers and in the pockets of big business, unless of course the facts bear this out. Indeed, he encourages his hearers to mortify their personal hatred of the President—something we evidently did not hear enough of under Bill Clinton and George W. Bush.[63]

In short, whatever the personal or private convictions of the biblical-political preacher, he seeks to bring politically divided Christians together. This he attempts by calling them to investigate the pertinent issues on the basis of scriptural principle (where possible), and by challenging them to do so in a way consistent with Christian ethics. These allow for a person's

---

63. No matter how wrong left-leaning Christians considered President Bush to be, they had a duty not only to respect him as their President but to love him as a professed brother in Christ (1 John 2:9–11). The rightful response was to pray for the President rather than to maul him (1 Tim 2:1–4, for more on which, go to www.7thref.org and the audio of my November 9, 2008, sermon "Prayer for the President Elect").

innocence until proven guilty and the discovery and exposure of the politics of personal destruction. The misrepresentation of hasty accusations is easy to promote, but well-nigh impossible to overturn completely. Onlooking parties tend to be either too lazy or unwilling to get to the truth. Regularly, its pursuit takes independent judgment and courage in the face of ostracism (verbal and otherwise). Crucial in regard to the pursuit is the refusal to accept the unexamined assumptions of the day; not least those that would claim that the left wing is using the notion of social conscience to seek the spoliation of the rich ("If I can't be rich, you can't be either"), when in fact many are no doubt genuinely grieved by the great inequalities of wealth; or that the right wing is callous about the poor, when in fact many sincerely believe that the best way to encourage the poor out of the poverty trap is by supporting individual responsibility.

By careful use and relevant application of the Word, the biblical-political preacher sees the possibility and grasps the opportunity to peel back layers of suspicion and mistrust creeping from society into the church. He hopes, with the passage of time, that the heightening of the ethics of political discourse within the church will become part of the church's role as salt and light in the politically divided context of the surrounding culture. The ecclesial witness the biblical-political preacher seeks to improve is not simply verbal but practical. He recognizes that it is not enough to encourage the cessation of political hostilities within the church; there must also be constructive cooperation in the diaconal work of the church across congregational and denominational lines.[64] Whatever directions Christians go thereafter in entering the public square, they at least do so from a shared investment in the message and ministry of the church, and in the particular localities and spheres to which they are called.

---

64. Note David Kuo's recent recommendation of this in his conclusion to *Tempting Faith*.

STUDY QUESTIONS

1. What is it about the current state of affairs in the world that burdens you most? Think locally, regionally, nationally, and internationally. Are there issues that should burden you more than they do?

2. What do you understand are the main features of the Bible's world-and-life view, and what relevance do they have to the challenges of the present culture war?

3. What place does the Bible's interest in "social righteousness" play in your preaching/the preaching you sit under? How do you envision the communication of this interest impacting the Christian contribution in society's ongoing culture war?

4. How does the Lordship of Christ over the conscience impinge on your response to the known political choices and action of Christian brothers and sisters within your congregation?

5. How can we exemplify trust in the sovereignty of God amid reversals in the culture war without giving off the impression that divine sovereignty is fatalism?

3

A Practical Way

The Application of the Biblical-Political Approach

> *If we mend our careless ways, perhaps we will become more sure-footed and sensible in our engagement with the public square. At least we may learn to speak to the people we find in it. God willing, we may learn to bring up from beneath those truths of general revelation that they cannot fail to know but can all too easily push down. We may even learn to whet that inexplicable longing that can ultimately be satisfied only by Christ himself.*
>
> —J. Budziszewski,
> *Evangelicals in the Public Square*

It is the wisdom of the biblical-political approach to maximize and extend Christian saltiness and light in the public square. Christians, we have noted, fulfill Christ's familiar metaphor by pursuing social transformation. This transformation requires us to be radically different from non-Christians, while nevertheless rubbing shoulders with them.[1] As preachers, ours is the responsibility to so expound the Word as to encourage our hearers to be in the world without being of it. To preach in this way, we must:

---

1. Stafford, "Evangelism Plus," 99.

1. BE PASSIONATE!

Whereas the apolitical are likely to perceive the biblical-political approach to extinguish passion for the celestial, the party-political will likely be impatient with what appears to be the biblical-political disinterest in the terrestrial. The reality is that the biblical-political are fired up by both, although they do not regard the terrestrial and the celestial as equally ultimate. Our goal in the final analysis is not victory in the culture war or freedom for the nations, but the glory of God in the consummation of his Kingdom. It is its invincible progress that ensures the supplemental blessings of domestic and social enrichment, as well as national freedom. The passion of the biblical-political preacher is, then, energetic and encompassing of the concerns of both the apolitical and party-political. Inspired by the Holy Spirit and controlled by Scripture, this passion is also measured in its expression.

2. BE FAITHFUL!

Faithfulness demands we prioritize our duties and our interests in line with the nature of our calling. If we wish to be overtly partisan or party-political, then let's stop claiming a call to preach and move into politics. Let's not mix the preached Word with party politics. But if pulpit ministry is our calling then we need to *preach* the Word and preach *the Word*![2] After all, faithful preach-

---

2. Regrettable in this regard is former presidential candidate Mike Huckabee's departure from the ministry of the Word. I was present at a Pastor's breakfast in Grand Rapids in early 2008 to hear him explain his transition to the realm of politics. Having been a pastor of a sizable congregation, chairman of Arkansas' Baptist State Convention (1989–91), and highly involved in pro-life overtures to his state government, he left what he described as his comfort zone on the advice of his family to pursue further the pro-life agenda.

Given the seriousness of the abortion issue, we can understand this

ing is the lifeblood of the church's ministry. By it we maintain our focus on the gospel, without pitting it against the social concerns of God. We achieve this balance through the broad (i.e., relevant) utilization of Scripture. By this utilization we are able to emerge from our ghettos without heading for party headquarters. This approach, however, can only work well if we heighten the profile of authentic exposition in the church, and exemplify its merit. Impressing upon the church the importance of biblical exposition will take both a high view and a high use of Scripture. This is achieved by faithful exegesis, sound hermeneutics, and a humble dependence on the Spirit, as well as by the utilization in pulpit ministry of a rich experience of life and a wide-ranging familiarity with different fields of knowledge. This knowledge cannot but serve to broaden and mature our application of the Word.

Of course, the knowledge of theology *and* politics (and life in general) is a tall order. But then that's exactly what ministry is! James Montgomery Boice is not entirely elitist or overly critical of seminaries when he states his conviction, "that those with the very best minds and training belong in the pulpit, and that the pulpit will never have the power it once had (and ought to have) until this happens."[3] I agree, in part, because pulpit ministry requires sufficient abilities to master the classics of both the church and the world, and the insight to enlist the latter in the service of the former. Writes Boice,

> Obviously the sermon is not a lecture. It is exposition of
> a text of Scripture in terms of contemporary culture with
> the specific goal of helping people to understand and

---

in part. Undoubtedly, Huckabee is an honest, winsome, and attractive Christian, who defends well the sanctity of life. Nonetheless, the whereabouts of his initial call to preach is a mystery; all the more so, now he has chosen to become a political commentator with Fox News Channel rather than return to pulpit ministry. In this regard Huckabee has traveled in the opposite direction of Ed Dobson (*Blinded by Might*, 19–24).

3. Boice, "The Preacher and Scholarship," 91.

obey the truth of God. But to do that well the preacher must be well studied. To do it exceptionally he must have exceptional understanding of (1) the Scripture he is expounding, (2) the culture into which he is expounding it, and (3) the spirituality and psychology of the people he is helping to obey God's Word. These understandings do not come merely from native abilities or mere observance of life. They come from hard study as the preacher explores the wisdom of both the past and the present to assist him in his task.[4]

Boice is likely right to say that we have forgotten the intellectual demands of the ministry.[5] It is easy to do so in an age wherein that which doesn't come easily, doesn't come. Yet our usefulness to the role our hearers play in the public square is at stake. As former British Prime Minister Margaret Thatcher (1979–90) once reminded a gathering of ministers in Scotland: Our "success" as preachers "matters greatly—as much to the temporal as to the spiritual welfare of the nation."[6] We need to take a lead, then, in fulfilling the role Maritain foresaw Christians could

---

4. Boice, "The Preacher and Scholarship," 91–92.

5. Nonetheless, the intellectual demands of ministry ought not to be pitted against its pastoral focus. There are great dangers in our Reformed circles of a lopsided cerebral approach lacking in pastoral warmth and care. Balance is necessary here as always. Capturing it is perhaps the toughest challenge for those with stellar intellectual abilities. What keeps the use of these abilities in harmony with the priorities of the perfect ministry of Christ is the maintenance of meaningful contact with our congregants. Pastoral interaction fuels love and care, as well as accuracy in the application of the Word. The current trend that has turned preaching into the reading of draft chapters of forthcoming books not only denies implicitly the primacy of preaching, it also raises sincere questions about the quality of pastoral care on offer. Our congregants are not to be used as spectators in a literary refinement process.

6. *Christianity & Conservatism*, 338.

play at the outset of the last world war; namely, the reconstruction of political philosophy and the rediscovery of God.[7]

This contribution is far more necessary in this third world war than it was in the last, now that the West no longer understands the necessity of integrating Christian values into the defense of our freedom.[8] The beauty of this contribution is that it is one we can develop without compromising the basis or nature of our calling. It entails the training up of Christians as front line troops who raise society's consciousness of God as a means of challenging the Western secularism so provocative to Islamic aggression.[9] To the party-political this response will appear very humdrum. And yet, for all the conferences and publication of books nowadays, this training up of Christians remains necessary and requires beefing up (hence the appeal for expository preaching). Notes Colson: "In the Kingdom of God one learns the obligations of citizenship from the Scriptures, the ultimate source of basic Christian truth. Unfortunately, many people, churched or unchurched, are woefully ignorant in this area." He continues: "If the average churchgoer is uninformed . . . one does not have to look far to understand why. Church leaders have treated us to a smorgasbord of trendy theologies, pop philoso-

---

7. "If the Western democracies are not to be swept away, and a night of long centuries is not to come down upon civilization, it is on condition that they discover in its primitive purity their vital principle, which is justice and love, and whose source is of divine origin. It is on condition that they reconstruct their political philosophy and thus rediscover the sense of justice and heroism in the rediscovery of God" (Maritain, *The Twilight of Civilization*, 45).

8. Maritain, *The Twilight of Civilization*, 39.

9. Writes Colson: "Though . . . the church's primary function is evangelization and ministering to spiritual needs; as the principle visible manifestation of the Kingdom of God, it must be the conscience of society, the instrument of moral accountability" (*God & Government*, 373; *cf.* 314 [Colson's quotation of the Southern Presbyterian theologian R. L. Dabney]).

phies, and religious egocentric cultural values."[10] Faithfulness requires us as preachers to speak in the first instance to the church, directing our members as to how they may serve society and extend Christ's Kingdom; they, by contrast, speak immediately to the world, including "the powers that be" (i.e., "the governing authorities" [Rom 13:1]). They do so in the ultimate hope of pointing them to Christ, and in the general hope of gaining respect for the wholesome Christian contribution to society.[11]

3. BE OBJECTIVE!

We preachers can only claim to be anchored to the Word when we are objective in its application. For the Word must always be applied on its own terms, without fearing or favoring one party over another. Campolo's even-handed measurement of the respective strengths and weaknesses of the traditional stances of the Republican and Democratic parties, suggests that this objectivity is possible, even though to many of our hearers it may be distasteful.[12] Many in conservative circles will wonder how the objective application of the Word can be anything other than pro-Republican. Understandably, they are concerned by the Democratic Party's "San Francisco values": policies of pro-choice and support for homosexual marriage (assuming the accuracy of a recent American Family Association Action Alert, etc.). These compare so negatively to the GOP's more general concern for traditional family values and the pro-life cause that an increasing number of preachers doubtless believe the biblical-political and party-political approaches to coincide; which is to say that the exposition of Scripture clearly favors the Republican Party agenda.

I do not deny that the Republican Party is closer overall to a number of the social issues that matter most to orthodox

10. Colson, *God & Government*, 276.
11. For more on this, see below (4. Be Responsible!).
12. Campolo, *Is Jesus Republican or Democrat?* 3–7.

Christians.[13] Indeed, I would counsel those described by one blogger's website as "Left of Calvary" to reflect earnestly on the issues of conscience that make it difficult for Christians to vote Democratic. Nevertheless, my instincts as an expositor tell me to wait a moment before uncritically concluding that the Republican Party is the political wing of the Christian church. Several reasons account for this hesitation.

First, I observe that the Republican stance on social issues does not bring Republicans necessarily any closer to God.[14] At one level—the political level—this does not matter so much. We vote on policy not on spirituality. Nonetheless, the inconsistencies of both party policy and party conduct, on top of the politically driven selection of ethical or moral policy choices explains why, "the red-blue split of weekly churchgoers has narrowed. Commentators," claims Kuo, "are atwitter about the shrinking of the 'God gap.'"[15]

Indeed, had Rudy Guiliani received the Republican Party's nomination for the 2008 Presidential election, how much difference would there have been between the social agendas of the two parties in the race for the White House? To this, Christian

---

13. A clear evidence of this was seen, for instance, in the Saddleback *Civil Forum* of August 2008 in the varied responses of Obama and McCain to the question of when life begins. Interestingly, Obama testified clearly to his trust in Christ as Savior but issued the deplorable claim that the question of the origin of life was "above his pay grade." McCain, by contrast, evidently operates from a privatized and erroneous (informally universalist) notion of Christian belief (see my earlier comment about his 2008 reception speech), but is crystal clear in his unwavering commitment to the view that life begins at conception.

14. "Scandals are not the exclusive property of Republicans or Democrats, though each party tries to cast itself as more moral than the other. Following a scandal involving one party, the other party promises to usher in a 'new era' of honesty and integrity. Somehow it never quite works out that way" (Thomas and Beckel, *Common Ground*, 126).

15. Kuo, "Putting Faith Before Politics."

Republicans may argue that Guiliani's failure to receive the nomination is evidence that there is a significant difference between the Republican and Democratic parties. Perhaps, maybe even probably; but the truth remains the same: both parties have elements from which Christians ought to stand back, if for no other reason than that "nearly 60 percent of non-evangelicals [now] have a more negative view of Jesus because of Christian political involvement."[16] After all, what are we to make of the Log Cabin Republicans and their potential for influencing party policy?[17] Of Kuo's claim in *Tempting Faith* that the Bush administration manipulated Evangelicals for its own ends? Or of the series of corruption scandals that dogged the late Republican administration (Jack Abramoff, Tom Delay,[18] former Senator Mark Foley, etc.)?

Secondly, I hesitate concluding that good exposition necessarily results in pro-Republicanism, because a narrow approach to the important issues of the day is often used to draw this conclusion. In the process, a political agenda can sometimes be imposed on the text of Scripture, while other texts or portions of God's Word deemed somewhat inconvenient fail to receive the attention they are due (e.g., the Sermon on the Mount). So while I do not underestimate the relevance of social issues to the welfare of the nation, and am left unconvinced that the secularizing

16. Kuo, "Putting Faith Before Politics."

17. Log Cabin Republicans are gay and lesbian. To learn more of their activity, go to their website "Log Cabin Republicans" and to the Wikipedia entry that goes under the same name.

18. Bipartisan coauthors Cal Thomas and Bob Beckel offer a pretty grim assessment of Tom Delay, describing him as "the most extreme partisan in Congress since Lyndon Johnson was majority leader in the Senate in the 1950s" (*Common Ground*, 149). "A former pest exterminator who treated Democrats the way he used to treat roaches," he was indicted by an admittedly Democratic Texas prosecutor for laundering campaign contributions and came under further suspicion because of his relationship to lobbyist Jack Abramoff, who had pled guilty to conspiracy to bribe members of Congress (ibid., 2).

elements of the Democratic Party have been dealt with merely because the party now draws on an array of theological leanings as broadly liberal as the politics of the party,[19] I caution against the assumption that the Bible is basically a pro-Republican text. The matter is just not that simple. For one thing, the Republican Party, taken as a whole, resonates a cultural Christianity as much as it does one that is biblical.

Take, for instance, the issue of the gun lobby. At face value the arguments supporting it seem strong. Amendment II of the Constitution, ratified effective December 15, 1791, states that "a well regulated Militia, being necessary to the security of a free State, the right of the people to keep and bear Arms, shall not be infringed." While the wording is clear, can anyone doubt that the context has changed? The amendment pre-dates the coast-to-coast settlement of the country, the establishment of the armed services as a regular standing force representative of the nation, and the founding of a regular police force. We pay our taxes for these services like any other country, only Americans do not trust their government or the services operative under its control to the extent that other democratic nations trust theirs.

Furthermore, it is stated rather pragmatically that the widespread availability of guns and the levels of violence make the right to bear arms an ongoing necessity. According to *The Philadelphia Inquirer*, between 2001 and March 2005, 6265 people were shot in the city, 17 percent of whom died. In 2004 there were only 11 days in which no one was shot.[20] Indeed, in 2005 there were an estimated 327 deaths from gunfire in Philadelphia (surpassed in 2006), while in 2007 there were 417 deaths in Detroit. Then, we may mention the string of massacres, which have become too numerous to enumerate. "Columbine" has become the euphemism for the wild-west element of American so-

---

19. Erroneous theologians no more safeguard the spiritual interests of orthodox Christians than do erroneous politicians.

20. Gorenstein, "Shootings."

ciety—which violent lawlessness is just about unique among the self-professed civilized nations of the earth. There is then some truth to the claim that citizens need guns of their own to defend themselves, and that armed crime is lower in incidents where commensurate self-defense is possible.

All the same there is something truly disheartening about this line of argument. It rules out too easily a thought—nay a hope—that is logically prior; namely, the disarming of the criminal community so that citizens don't have to defend themselves militarily. "It can't be done!", goes up the cry. But is it not strange that we find no difficulty in believing we can send one wave of armed forces after another across the other side of the world to disarm tyrants, rebels, and their henchmen, but claim helplessness in disarming the criminal community under our own noses? This argument seems to me all the more unconvincing when we consider that terrorists have killed far fewer Americans than have the Republic's own citizens!

Please don't misunderstand me! I am not calling for the easing up on terrorists, nor am I seeking the end of recreational hunting. I am merely pointing out the double standard, which seems to be born of an inability or an unwillingness to look objectively at the problems and sins of our own society. This blind patriotism and the double standard it allows are possible because of the general lack of resolve to deal with the gun problem. Does not the fear of even the slightest tightening of the gun laws drive the argument? The regrettable political reality is that conflict on foreign soil inspires patriotism, stories of heroism, and won elections, while talk of measures that could inhibit gun use (even to a limited degree) results in a defensive maintenance of the status quo.

So the killings and massacres go on, and are aided by the constitutional second amendment and, in this context, the convenient idolization of the notion of limited government. The result is that an otherwise great country and leading democracy tolerates a barbarism symbolized by the no-go areas of the country. We preachers can certainly support the civil government in its policies of containment and penalization, but there's more we can do. In the course of expounding Scripture, we can teach that the notion of "an eye for an eye and a tooth for a tooth" (Exod 21:24; Lev 24:20; Deut 19:21) was actually a primitive form of policing in Old Testament times. Those of our hearers who have bought into the gun lobby's pragmatic line of argument may want to be reminded of our Lord's revision of this Old Testament principle:

> You have heard that it was said, "An eye for an eye and a tooth for a tooth." But I tell you not to resist an evil person. But whoever slaps you on your right cheek, turn the other to him also. If anyone wants to sue you and take away your tunic, let him have your cloak also. And whoever compels you to go one mile, go with him two. Give to him who asks you, and from him who wants to borrow from you do not turn away. You have heard that it was said, "You shall love your neighbor and hate your enemy." But I say to you, love your enemies, bless those who curse you, do good to those who hate you, and pray for those who spitefully use you and persecute you, that you may be sons of your Father in heaven; for He makes His sun rise on the evil and on the good, and sends rain on the just and on the unjust. (Matt 5:38–45).

When these biblical principles come to shape Christian thinking, those of us who query this Republican "no brainer" may cease to be dismissed as "social liberals."[21] Such ill-con-

---

21. Hope for a sea-change of opinion remains slim at present. Recently the Supreme Court passed a ruling confirming the right to hold weapons in the District of Columbia. The ruling was widely proclaimed to have nationwide significance. Two familiar features of the right-wing response have been present: the greater readiness to speak of constitutional rights than of the frequency of massacres; the excusing of the prioritization of the talk of rights by allusion to statistics demonstrating that gun crime is less in cases where the innocent are armed. The disarming of the criminal community appears not to be an

ceived judgments are not only parochial (influenced in part by American isolation), they are evidence of how much history and culture encroach on our Christian perception of things.

Thirdly, I hesitate equating biblical exposition with the Republican agenda because of the evident mistakes of the last eight years of the Republican administration, and the knock-on effect of these mistakes on the way the church is perceived. I fear that if we continue to assume that the Bible is pro-Republican we shall hold back from indicting the sins of the Republican Party, and thereby lose the prophetic element of our preaching. Let's take the well-documented blunders of the second Iraq war as our example.

Accepting that the overall war on terror was necessary and that President Bush—by all appearances a good man—waged

---

option for discussion or planning.

Whatever the ugliness of the antisocial behavior in Britain—and it is ugly and depressing—it is worth pointing out by contrast how rare are the massacres there. There have been but two in my lifetime: those at Hungerford in England (1987) and Dunblane in Scotland (1996). The former "remains, along with the Dunblane massacre, one of the worst criminal atrocities involving firearms in British history" (http://en.wikipedia.org/wiki/Hungerford_massacre). The first massacre (sixteen deaths and fifteen wounded) led to the Firearms (Amendment) Act of 1988, banning the ownership of semi-automatic center-fire rifles and restricting the use of shotguns with a magazine capacity of more than two rounds. The second (sixteen children and one adult killed) led to the Firearms (Amendment) (No. 2) Act 1997, which banned remaining .22 cartridge handguns in England, Scotland, and Wales (omitting Northern Ireland, the Isle of Man, and the Channel Islands). This left only muzzle-loading and historic hand guns legal, as well as certain sporting handguns (e.g., "Long Arms"). These restrictions have not only prevented another massacre to date, they have ensured that the police on the streets of Britain remain unarmed. It goes without saying that the human heart is no different in Britain, as is evident in the recent rise of knife crime, but the legislation has to date successfully limited opportunities for its deadly outworking. It is uncertain what tragedy it will take in America for the public to question the present malaise.

the Iraqi conflict with the best of intentions, we may nevertheless ask whether a second Iraq war was the way to go after 9/11. Americans influenced by homegrown pragmatism ("If it works it must be right") tend to justify the war on the basis of whether it has been successful, rather than by determining whether it was morally right or wrong. While President Bush was successful in ensuring that America enjoyed safety during the rest of his presidency, and has been admirable in the face of his many critics in awaiting the verdict of history, we would be naïve to think that success (e.g., the removal of Saddam Hussein) justifies morally inadequate decisions and the administration's inadequate preparation for this latest "peace."[22] Given that tens and tens of thousands have lost their lives, each fatality made in the image of God, it simply does not do to ignore the question of the morality of the war, or to dismiss the estimates of fatalities as hyped up or merely a fact of war.[23] Even Saddam would have taken some time to match them! Nor dare we justify the claims concerning the secret camps, and the allegations of torture at Guantanamo Bay. We insist, rather, that an ethical conflict be waged not only for the right reasons, but in the right way.

22. Saddam's capture, trial, and execution cannot justify the death toll. Only the successful stabilization (democratization) of Iraq can begin to do that, so long as the resettlement of the country is accompanied by long-lasting peace dividends for the world. Despite the success of the surge, it may take as long as fifty years to judge this, and even then such a judgment could only guess at how things would have been without a second Iraq war.

23. I have no axe to grind against the British and American governments. Like so many, I trusted their judgment and decency, but cannot make light of the estimates. These vary from 70,000 to 655,000 (the first figure is Bob Beckel's, drawn from Thomas and Beckel, *Common Ground*, 156, the second from a U.S. survey). While many of these deaths are due to the tribal conflict present in the country and the imported influence of *Al Qaeda*, it is well nigh impossible to deny that it was the war and the subsequent political vacuum that sparked the post-war violence in Iraq.

This insistence may require not only the negation of the Republican Party but also the right-wing pundits. We may question, for example, the typically sane voice of Cal Thomas, whose rather pragmatic assessment of the Iraq War is based on old rather than new covenant principle:

> If our good behavior made our enemies behave like us, I would say let's be better than we are. But it doesn't and so the only way to win—if winning is our goal (anything less is defeat)—is to outdo them. Does that offend? It offends me more to have these people jerk our chain. It offends me more to wait for the next attack, preceded by an ultimatum issued by hundreds of people who illegally entered our country, or who may have been born here and were radicalized in Wahaabi schools subsidized by the Saudi Arabian government, our "ally" in the war on terror.[24]

We appreciate Thomas's concerns, but have a responsibility nevertheless to let Scripture dictate our responses.

One of the benefits that comes with being objective is a sensitivity to those brothers and sisters in the Lord who vote differently than we do. The cause of the varied voting pattern may be a difference in background, of geographical location, and therefore of historical molding. As a Welshman studying in Scotland during the 1990s, for instance, I was initially bemused, but gradually disturbed, to witness hostility directed against Christians from southern England (south of Watford Gap). The marked variation of accent seemed to indicate the significant difference of political outlook. Tensions ran especially high during the Thatcher years. I vividly recall the day when a brother in Christ rushed into the student common room exclaiming her downfall: "She's gone! She's gone!" A lightening rod she may have been, and certainly the Poll Tax finished her off in Scotland, but

---

24. Thomas and Beckel, *Common Ground*, 160.

was it really appropriate for Christians to speak of her as if they hated her?[25] Whatever her standing before God, it is worth noting she had in her cabinet a Christian Lord Chancellor (Lord Mackay), while her successor John Major had another, Brian Mawhinney. Obviously their Christianity could not ensure good government, but it does raise the question as to whether the Christian participation in the Left's hatred of Mrs. Thatcher was justified. I am not saying that Thatcherism got everything right, but neither should we be disposed to believe that the "Iron Lady" got everything wrong. Far from it! It is worth asking whether the United Kingdom has benefited from her sudden departure.

In short, we preachers practice sensitivity when we point our more partisan hearers toward a fresh sympathetic-critical (objective) attitude to the party of their choice; at least to the extent that Scripture deems a more open approach appropriate. Sympathetic criticism breeds honesty about the failures of our own preferred political tradition, and ensures that the party manifesto does not gain the same standing as Scripture. It also keeps us from naively assuming that members of the government/administration or opposition are necessarily doing God's bidding. Even supposing they are, we dare not assume in the murky nature of politics that they are going about it in a way pleasing to God.[26]

---

25. Those Christian readers still tempted to hate Mrs. Thatcher may be challenged by her famous "Sermon on the Mound" (a pun cross-referencing Jesus' sermon on the mount with Mrs. Thatcher's 1988 speech to the General Assembly of the Church of Scotland, delivered on "The Mound" [a parochial reference to Mound Place, the location of the Hall of the General Assembly]). The speech is included in *Christianity & Conservatism*, 333–38.

26. I am not meaning to be cynical, for civil government is God's invention. Indeed, Colson may well be right to interpret Paul to say that "even a bad government is a better alternative than no government—which results in chaos" (*God & Government*, 373). Nevertheless, the operations of civil government in a fallen context alert us to the need for

4. BE RESPONSIBLE!

Although we preachers are not, typically, to desert our calling, we nevertheless have a responsibility to fulfill our civic duties, and to call our congregants to do the same.[27] Bonhoeffer's words of long ago retain relevance for the present: "The Church must get out of her stagnation. We must move out again into the open air of intellectual discussion with the world, and risk shocking people if we are to cut any ice."[28] This is urgent, and the longer we procrastinate in encouraging our hearers to leave the ghetto, the more difficult it becomes. Notes Schaeffer:

> The people in the United States have lived under the Judeo-Christian consensus for so long that now we take it for granted. We seem to forget how completely unique what we have had is a result of the gospel. . . . We have forgotten why we have a high view of life, and why we have a positive balance between form and freedom in government, and the fact that we have such tremendous freedoms without these freedoms leading to chaos. Most of all, we have forgotten that none of these is natural to the world. They are unique, based on the fact that the consensus was the biblical consensus. And these things will be even further lost if this other total view, the materialistic view, takes over more thoroughly. We can be certain that what we so carelessly take for granted will be lost.[29]

---

realism. Realistic expectations of civil government, if appropriated well, can promote an intentional reflection of the values and grace of Christ in the political discourse of our flocks.

27. Bopp writes: "Churches may engage in non-partisan voter registration, voter identification, get out the vote, and voter education activities so long as such activities are not intended at the supporters of any particular candidate or political party" ("Do's and Don'ts for Political Activities of Pastors").

28. Bonhoeffer, *Letters & Papers from Prison*, 128.

29. *A Christian Manifesto* in *The Complete Works*, 5:455–56.

The moral and spiritual collapse of Great Britain clearly illustrates that our American cousins did not suffer this amnesia first nor, to date, most severely. Despite Britain's obvious secularism, only recently have Anglicans holding high office—so privileged on the one hand but so at sea on the other—begun to send forth anything like a certain sound. One example of this has been the recent condemnation by the Archbishop of York, Dr. John Sentamu, of what he calls "the systematic erosion of Christianity from public life." Complaining that illiberal atheists are undermining Britain's religious heritage, he adds that, "Christians should be more politically active to ensure their principles were [sic] not purged from society."[30]

While we may not tell our congregations which way to vote, urging our hearers to cast their ballot is a given to many. Participation in the electoral process is one way faithful Christians can be salt and light. The 67 percent of Evangelicals who, it is said, passed up the opportunity to exercise their vote in the 2000 U.S. Presidential election missed out on a convenient way to make their voice heard. Apparently they made up for it in 2004.[31] But it is worth remembering that a candidate's Christian credentials do not guarantee that she/he will be a better politician and achieve more than his/her morally upstanding opponent. We recall that, in God's common providence, decent unbelievers contributed much to the building of Western society (albeit within a Judeo-Christian frame of reference).

Just as objectivity attracts sensitivity, so responsibility demands wisdom. This is especially necessary in discerning and

---

30. During the same week, the Archbishop of Canterbury, Rowan Williams, and Catholic leader Cardinal Cormac Murphy-O'Connor launched a joint attack on what they called intolerant public atheism ("Archbishop attacks public atheism").

31. It is said that "self-identified evangelicals provided almost 40% of Mr Bush's vote in 2004; if you add in the other theological conservatives, such as Mormons and traditional Catholics, that number rises closer to 60%." ("In the World of Good and Evil," 37).

advocating the difference between our role in the culture war and that of our hearers. We may speak in an immediate sense chiefly to the church, but they speak chiefly and directly to the world. In doing so, they face the challenge of navigating the thorny issues of the Constitution and the use of divine revelation.

The founding fathers would doubtless be shocked to learn, were they with us today, how contentious is the Constitution's separation of the church and state: "Congress shall make no law respecting an establishment of religion, or prohibiting the free exercise thereof" (Amendment I, ratified December 15, 1791). Not only did they assume theism, they worked within a generally accepted Judeo-Christian framework.[32] Accordingly, their use of the term "religion" was not intended to silence the church but to deny the establishment of one national church, and to prevent the government from interfering with the free practice of religion.[33] In the current pluralistic age, secular progressives seek to isolate the wording of the Constitution from its context, thereby arguing for the termination of the privileged position of Christianity.

In responding to this challenge, we preachers have a responsibility to distinguish for our hearers the essential liberties of the church from her historic privileges. Whereas the former are assumed under the Constitution, the latter are not, other than in some general sense shared by theists. Those American Christians not liking this must, if they are to be consistent, jettison their voluntaryist notion of church-state relations in favor of the Establishment principle, and amend the Constitution so that it becomes unequivocally and specifically pro-Christian. Realistically speaking, however, they are best following Schaeffer's advice:

---

32. As Richard Brookhiser has written, "If the founders did not make America a Christian nation, many of them thought it should be a religious nation. In their view religions sustained the civic culture of the state" (*What Would the Founders Do?* 65).

33. Schaeffer, *A Christian Manifesto* in *The Complete Works*, 5:433–34.

> As we stand for religious freedom today, we need to realize that this must include a general religious freedom from the control of the state for all religion. It will not just mean freedom for those who are Christians. It is then up to Christians to show that Christianity is the Truth of total reality in the open marketplace of freedom.[34]

We should not be overly concerned about this. The "fortunes" of Christianity rest, we must remember, not so much on its preferential treatment by the state, as on its innate superiority as a system of belief. This superiority is rooted in the supernatural content of the faith, especially as it finds climactic expression in the person and work of the Lord Jesus Christ. While evading elitism, we Christians ought not to shy away from either believing or expressing wisely the uniqueness of Christianity.

That said, the vested interest of the secular progressives in the separation of the church and state (often as a cover for the excising of Christ from culture), compounded by the desire that America follow the path of Western European secularism, raises significant questions as to how we utilize divine revelation for the spread of the gospel and the redemption of society.

Obviously, we preachers major within the church on the communication of special revelation (Holy Scripture). For Christians need to know what they believe and must be able and willing to speak up for Christ in the public square, wherever and whenever it is appropriate to do so. This is Plan A. Writes John Frame:

> I wouldn't say . . . that we should enter the public arena slinging Bible verses in every direction. But I do believe that God's entire revelation gives us the only objective truth available in any area of human life or thought. There is no room for autonomous human thought in any realm of life; such thought will inevitably fail. We need to take our standards from Scripture. And if it

---

34. Ibid., 5:440.

> helps occasionally to actually quote Scripture, we should
> be unashamed to do that.[35]

Yet, when we preach and teach Scripture competently, we cannot help but stress to our hearers the validity and usefulness of general revelation.[36] What we teach them about general revelation can be put to use in the public square at any time, but will have to be by faithful witnesses where and when there is resistance to Plan A. It is worth us remembering that the rejection of the gospel (Plan A) does not preclude us from making progress by means of Plan B: the application of general revelation in areas commonly shared among believers and unbelievers alike. While Plan B is less than ideal when compared with Plan A, it is nevertheless useful, especially in an environment ill-disposed toward Christians. "When people are closed to special revelation," writes Budziszewski, "the only possible appeal is to general revelation, to the things we can't *not* know."[37]

A pragmatic approach this may be, but not entirely so. It is God who has given us general revelation. In it he has made natural law evident to Christians and to non-Christians alike (Rom. 1:18–21; 2:12–16). Indeed, it is for our flocks, urged on effectively

---

35 "Reflections," 1:5.

36. General revelation is the "divine disclosure to all persons at all times by which one comes to know that God is, and what he is like" (Demarest, "Revelation, General," 944). Besides communicating basic elements of God's existence and character (Rom 1:18–21), it explains man's universal internal possession of the moral law (by which he is able to distinguish good and evil); it gives believing and unbelieving men and women some common ground in the discussion of matters pertinent to the faith and the public square (the knowledge of God and of his law); it provides the rational basis for God's saving revelation mediated through Jesus Christ. "In this sense," writes Demarest, "natural theology [general revelation] serves as the vestibule of revealed theology" ("Revelation, General," 945). Only in special revelation ("revealed theology") are such saving truths as the Trinity, incarnation, and atonement imparted.

37. Budziszewski, *Evangelicals in the Public Square*, 85.

by the worldview disseminated through our consecutive exposition of Scripture, to retrieve the usefulness of general revelation for the defense and advance of principles dear to Christians. Writes Budziszewski:

> Many Evangelicals are unfamiliar with the concept of general revelation. Evangelical theologians are somewhat reluctant to say much about it, not because they think it isn't real—as we have just seen, Scripture itself testifies to its reality—but because they fear that saying much about it might detract from the more perfect revelation of the Bible.[38]

In encouraging the retrieval of general revelation Budziszewski makes another valuable point we preachers would do well to pass on:

> We should not beat unbelievers over the head with general revelation any more than we should do so with special revelation. The line "Natural law says!" is no more persuasive, by itself, than the line "The Bible says!" But we need not invoke the natural law tradition by name just to make use of it. What the Christian natural law tradition teaches us is what nonbelievers, in fragmentary fashion, already know—whether or not they *know* that they know it, whether or not they *think* that they know it, and even if they would rather *not* know it. Viewed this way, the art of the cultural apologetic is less a matter of laying foundations than of digging up and repairing them, less a matter of talking people into truths they do not yet know than of dredging up what they do know but have not acknowledged.[39]

Consistent with our congregants' focus on general revelation is their apologetic use of the inalienable human rights we

38. Ibid., 31.
39. Ibid., 37.

share in common with our peers across society. As Schaeffer notes, the founding fathers of America could not have spoken of these had they not believed law (as opposed to the monarch) was king. Law can only be king because there is a Lawgiver.[40] In a climate, therefore, in which the principles and hegemony of Christianity may no longer be welcome, we may nevertheless contribute to what we see as the welfare of society by appealing to our right to be theists. We may also point out the value of Christianity to the welfare of the state, especially given the secular-progressive attempt to use Islamo-fascism as a smokescreen behind which to oppose all religion except their own religion of rationalism. What we Christians have lost in Europe and could lose in America in terms of social kudos (the privilege of belonging to a so-called Christian nation), we can yet make up for by means of evangelistic and apologetic effectiveness. Motivating our public testimony is the thought not only of repelling the forces of secular-progressiveness in the West, but of fulfilling our divine charge to promote Christ's Kingdom—a Kingdominion spread throughout the earth, the glory of which surpasses that of any earthly superpower.

5. BE CREATIVE!

In the years ahead, we preachers will need to be more outspoken in encouraging political involvement. Understandably, Schaeffer chastens Christian lawyers of the period 1940–70 for not blowing the whistle on changes to the Judeo-Christian basis of law, spe-

---

40. Schaeffer, *A Christian Manifesto* in *The Complete Works*, 5:432. In the church or the Kingdom of God, we recognize God to be the King and Lawgiver for all. Writes Colson: "This does not mean that the Old Testament's civic code should be passed by modern governments. What it does mean, as Plato and Cicero recognized, is that there are moral absolutes that must govern human behavior; there is a law rooted in truth upon which the laws of human society are based" (*God & Government*, 274).

cifically as they related to abortion.[41] We trust today's Christian lawyers are fighting against euthanasia and other social evils. Stating the principle in more general terms, we preachers face the task of teaching our congregations to diversify the fulfillment of their civic responsibilities. Writes Campolo:

> We need a new kind of politics that on the local level calls together churches, community organizations, indigenous leaders, and government officials. Local people working together can best understand and address the problems they encounter in their own neighborhoods.[42]

The packaging of policies along party lines and the current levels of bipartisan corruption makes party-political voting a fraught issue. The reality is that no party is the arm of the church. The underlying ideologies of the major British parties, for instance, have all felt some Christian influence;[43] but other factors have now come into play that lend greater importance to the individual candidate. These include the loss of the parties' ideological connection (notably in the nonsocialist tendencies of New Labour), the delegated nature of democracy, and the number of free votes available on issues of conscience. Accordingly, it is appropriate that church leaders make available information about the candidates in particular,[44] ensuring that the informa-

---

41. Schaeffer, *A Christian Manifesto* in *The Complete Works*, 5:440–42.

42. Campolo, *Is Jesus Republican or Democrat?* 13.

43. British Conservatism has historically been influenced by various strands of thought. I am thinking here of its theological strand, wherein the fall of man was said to argue for gradual rather than revolutionary change. In socialism, the notion of equality is rooted, historically, in the equal standing human beings have before God. As for Liberalism, its focus on individualism can be traced back to the popularity the notion gained at the time of the Reformation. This resulted from discussions of how a person can be right in the sight of God.

44. Bopp writes: "A church may distribute a voter guide regarding

tion we seek out is well-researched, fair, and gathered evenhandedly. As we've seen, it is not for the church to promote half-truths, outright lies, or smear campaigns.

But the ballot box is our least contribution, not our greatest. There are other ways, too, we may encourage civic involvement. Christian think tanks and lobby groups are likely to achieve more in the public square than can be accomplished individually. In the United Kingdom, the church could benefit from more organizations like the Christian Institute, the motto of which is "Christian influence in a secular world."[45] Our combined prayerful and financial support of them is the means of ensuring that their voices are heard more loudly. While this involvement might not be enough for the party-political, we ought not to underestimate the value of issue-driven Christian protest. A recent article on American foreign policy in the British magazine *The Economist* notes, surprisingly sympathetically, that "Christians are at the forefront of attempts to make American foreign policy more ethical." Supporting the idea that Christians are able to make a nonpolarizing and nonpolarized contribution to the culture war, the author continues:

> Evangelicals have campaigned against sex-trafficking and drug-trafficking, against poverty and religious persecution, and against the genocide in Sudan. They have led the charge to deal with AIDS in Africa (the person who did most to persuade Mr Bush to pledge $15 billion to that cause was his former chief speech-writer, an evangelical who has been dubbed "the conscience of the White House"). A group of leading evangelicals recently signed a statement on climate change proclaiming that

---

candidates' positions on various issues or a scorecard reporting on the voting records of incumbents. In such publications, the church or pastor may *not* state whether the candidate's vote is consistent with the church's" ("Do's and Don'ts for Political Activities of Pastors").

45. For more information, go to www.christian.org.uk.

> the problem is real, that human activity is an important cause, that the costs of inaction are high, and that those costs are disproportionately borne by the poor.[46]

On the home front, the signing of petitions and the writing of letters is becoming increasingly necessary, but it is encouraging that Christians are waking up to their responsibilities. It is in the writing of these that we have an opportunity to argue for the Christian cause, even if pragmatically; that is, along lines of natural law and common sense rather than by quoting, necessarily so, biblical text or verse. Given that "the pen is mightier than the sword," who knows how God will use our letters and action to improve society and to create thereby the best environment for the gospel to flourish and its spiritual and social advantages to be seen. Is not the Christian action of the eighteenth- and nineteenth-century Britain a stellar witness in this regard? A (re-)reading of the lives of William Wilberforce (1759–1833), Lord Shaftesbury (1801–85), George Müller (1805–98), Florence Nightingale (1820–1910), William Booth (1829–1912), and a host of others ought to inspire us today, and no doubt does inspire Christians already sociopolitically engaged.[47] Thinking specifically of Wilberforce and Lord Shaftesbury, Colson writes: "Christians who are politicians can bear a biblical witness on political structures, just as other professionals do in medicine, law, business, labor, education, the arts, or any other walk of life."[48] We preachers need to uphold such workers with biblical-political comment, aimed at encouraging and guiding them in their daily work.

---

46. "In the World of Good and Evil," 38.

47. Writes D'Souza, "however paradoxical it seems, people who believed most strongly in the next world did the most to improve the situation of people living in this one" (*What's So Great About Christianity Today?* 65). For relevant comment on the work of Wilberforce, see Colson, *God & Government*, 106 ff.

48. Colson, *God & Government*, 318.

Presently, we have reason to fear the threat party-political preachers pose the church's liberty. The forces arrayed against the church are bound to react sooner or later to the illegitimate use of the pulpit. Reactions to George Bush's overtly (crusading) Christian presidency could be just the start.[49] The last thing we need is a generation turned away from Christ by preachers who took a party-political stance in the pulpit. By the same token, it seems wholly inappropriate for apolitical ministers to enjoy the freedom they have to preach while standing silently by as that liberty is being eroded. The biblical-political approach alone can effectively promote spiritual growth and unity within the church, while enhancing the effectiveness of the church's witness in society. It is the only option of the three that enables the preacher to operate fully and relevantly as an ambassador of Christ (2 Cor 5:20; Eph 6:19). As such the biblical-political preacher reminds his hearers, in the words of Schaeffer, that

> . . . our culture, society, government, and law are in the condition they are in, *not because of a conspiracy, but because the church has forsaken its duty to be the salt of the culture.* It is the church's duty (as well as its privilege) to do now what it should have been doing all the time—to use the freedom we do have to *be* that salt of the culture. If the slide toward authoritarianism is to be reversed we need a committed Christian church that is dedicated to what John W. Whitehead calls "total revolution in the reformative sense."[50]

---

49. While, from a spiritual standpoint, there was something very appealing about President Bush's open profession of faith in Christ, I wonder whether his witness as President would have been more effective had he been more tactful, although not in such a Nicodemist fashion as Reagan. While I do not believe that Bush's public profession of faith has been politically driven, eternity will reveal to what degree it has been pragmatic.

50. Schaeffer, *A Christian Manifesto* in *The Complete Works*, 5:447.

STUDY QUESTIONS

1. What is the character of your Christian passion? For the heavenly in isolation from the earthly, for the earthly at the expense of the heavenly, or for the earthly with a view to the heavenly? Discuss.

2. How much do you seek to "know the times" (Rom 13:11), and what have you been learning about connecting the content of the Word to the context of the age?

3. Does the method of preaching you use/sit under allow for the exposition of the importance of general revelation in Christian theology? How may we use it without dumbing down the importance we place on special revelation?

4. How can we encourage each other to function effectively as theists without losing sight of the uniqueness of the Christian faith?

5. What practical ideas can you think of to influence the defense and preservation of Judeo-Christian values in your locality, region, and nation?

Conclusion

If a preacher is to be effective, he has to be convinced that Christ is Lord of the street corner and the marketplace as well as of the cathedral.

—Catherine Marshall,
A Man Called Peter[1]

So much more could be said. But this was never intended to be an exhaustive treatment of the nexus between the pulpit and the political realm. The study constitutes rather a tract for our times; a protest if you like, urging some rethinking by the church in her response to the culture war. Born of a particular moment of history, my point has been straightforward. Only a commitment to mature and consecutive exposition can recapture the significance of pulpit ministry for the public square. For by addressing what David Kinnaman rightly calls the "primary problem we are facing in Christianity today"—namely "superficial Christianity"[2]—expository preaching relevantly applied builds up the church in both internal strength and external effectiveness.

1. Marshall, *A Man Called Peter*, 37. My use of the prayers of Peter Marshall in the frontispiece, here, and in Appendix A, is not intended to suggest that his sermons are a model of biblical-political preaching, for they constitute colorful, devotional homilies rather than expository sermons. Nonetheless, there was something truly prophetic about Marshall's ministry, the tone of which is captured by his biblical-political prayers.

2. Kinnaman, "unChristian."

In making this claim, I am not blind to the complex nature of the relationship between the church and politics. Rick Warren alluded to this complexity in August 2008 when introducing his nationally televised *Civil Forum*. The separation of the church and state, he began, does not mean the separation of faith from politics.[3] Indeed, it is in the understanding of this distinction that we preachers have an opportunity to engage the culture war, but on God's terms.

To stimulate further thought and discussion I end with a brief enumeration of the salient points made:

1. We preachers ought to be most impassioned about the affairs of God's world, and especially for the generation and the place to which we have been divinely called.

2. Our chief task is to preach the Word of God into the church, and through the church into God's world in the name of Christ, by the power of the Holy Spirit, and for God's glory.

3. We preach most faithfully when we expound the whole scope of inscripturated revelation. While the Bible has chief relevance for the people of God—given its major focus on the blessings that come from the Father, through Christ, and by the Holy Spirit (Eph 1:3–14)—Scripture nevertheless contains socio-political implications relevant to the ongoing culture war.

4. We need to encourage the norm of an "educated ministry" capable of the in-depth study of the Word of God and of the prevailing times, and the connection of the one to the other.

---

3. Hynes writes: "The blending of religion and politics became necessary because the Democratic Party, which came to dominate America's political scene, lost touch with the nation's Christian roots and grew distant from a huge segment of the population that had grown increasingly religious and active in the imposition of their morality on its secular government" (*In Defense of the Religious Right*, 72).

5. Regardless of whether we have an ideological or party-political preference, we must expound Scripture at all times by means of the Bible's agenda alone.

6. The consecutive exposition of Scripture, fairly and maturely undertaken (the *bene esse* of preaching), lends objectivity to our ministries. Neither falling short of Scripture, nor going beyond it, our comments will sometimes favor one side of the political spectrum and sometimes another, depending on the passage at hand and the leanings and policies of the political parties in action at any given time. It is our Kingdom-centered objectivity that sets us apart from media analysts.

7. By consecutively expounding and applying Scripture, we preachers aim at the formation of a biblical world-and-life view within the minds, hearts, and lives of our hearers.

8. Critical to this biblical world-and-life view is the welfare and advancement of the Kingdom of Heaven. The fortunes of this Kingdom take precedence over party progress and national glory, although the pursuit of the Kingdom serves best the human race.

9. Our encouragement of political involvement aims chiefly to procure and sustain a context in which the gospel of God's Kingdom flourishes best.

10. The flourishing of the gospel not only saves souls, it tends toward the moralizing of the lost, with knock-on economic and social benefits for society.

11. Whereas our main focus as preachers is on special revelation (supremely Holy Scripture), our hearers are at liberty to draw more generally on general revelation in contexts where arguments from special revelation carry minimal weight in the unbelieving mind. The value and limitations of general revelation are found in the Word the preacher expounds. Its use has, therefore, biblical warrant.

12. The political involvement of our hearers can take a variety of forms, and need not be party-political or even party focused. Christians may find less conflict in working through think tanks and/or lobby groups, not to mention the diaconal work of the church. The decision as to whether to vote, and what to vote, is a matter of conscience—conscience informed by the Word of God.

13. Christians working at any level within the political sphere retain an obligation to function as salt and light, reflecting Christ not only in their commitment to truth but also to grace.

Operating from these principles, we preachers become critical to the winning of the culture war while becoming less of a liability to the church. For the biblical-political approach enables us to engage seriously the culture war, yet without disengaging from the war that is spiritual. A godly contribution to the culture war requires spiritual warfare. Indeed, we do not fight the Christian warfare to the full until we apply its strategies to the battle for culture. Whichever battle we emphasize at any given moment in ministry, the vision is the same: to see Christ stand victorious on the battlefield of time, and to do so as a divine agent of change that is eternal.

Ours is not a responsibility to sit and dream about this victory, but to stand and fight for it. Our weapons are spiritual, most prominent among which is not only the sermon, but prayer. It is with the latter we close, courtesy of Peter Marshall:

> We know, our Father, that at this desperate hour in world affairs, we need Thee. We need Thy strength, Thy guidance, Thy wisdom.
>
> There are problems far greater than any wisdom of man can solve. What shall our leaders do in such an hour.

May Thy wisdom and Thy power come upon the President of these United States, the Senators and Congressmen, to whom have been entrusted leadership. May the responsibility lie heavily on their hearts, until they are ready to acknowledge their helplessness and turn to Thee. Give to them the honesty, the courage, and the moral integrity to confess that they don't know what to do. Only then can they lead us as a nation beyond wisdom to Thee, who alone hast the answer.

Lead us to this high adventure. Remind us that a "mighty fortress is our God"—not a hiding place where we can escape for an easy life, but rather an arsenal of courage and strength—the mightiest of all, who will march beside us unto the battle for righteousness and world brotherhood.

O our God, may we never recover from our feeling of helplessness and our need of Thee! In the strong name of Jesus, our Lord, we pray. Amen.[4]

What Marshall prayed for the United States half a century ago, I pray today also for the United Kingdom. Amen ("Let it be") and amen!

---

4. *The Prayers of Peter Marshall*, 97.

Appendix A

AMERICA CONFESSES

PETER MARSHALL (1902–49), erstwhile Minister of New York Avenue Presbyterian Church, Washington D.C., and two-time Chaplain of the U.S. Senate, gave good expression throughout his ministry to this loyal, seeing, or objective patriotism. In illustrating this claim we can do no better than quote his sermon "The American Dream":

> There are so many things that are wonderful about America—things that are gloriously right and well worth defending. But there are also things that are deeply and dangerously wrong with America, and the true patriot is he who sees them regrets them and tries to remove them.[1]

This balance Marshall struck in prayer as well as in preaching. The following is titled "America Confesses":

Our Father, bring to the remembrance of Thy people Thine ancient and time-honored promise: 'If my people, which are called by my name, shall humble themselves, and pray, and seek my face, and turn from their wicked ways; then will I hear from heaven, and will forgive their sin, and will heal their land.'

May all of America come to understand that right-living alone exalteth a nation, that only in Thy will can peace and joy be found. But, Lord, this land cannot be righteous unless her people ar righteous, and we, here gathered, are part of America. We know the

1. Marshall, *A Man Called Peter*, 294.

world cannot be changed until the hearts of men are changed. Our hearts need to be changed.

We therefore confess to Thee that:

Wrong ideas and sinful living have cut us off from Thee.

We have been greedy.

We have sought to hide behind barricades of selfishness; shackles have imprisoned the great heart of America.

We have tried to isolate ourselves from the bleeding wounds of a blundering world.

In our self-sufficiency we have sought not Thy help.

We have conferences and ignored Thee completely.

We have disguised selfishness as patriotism; our arrogance has masqueraded as pride.

We have frittered away time and opportunities while the world bled.

Our ambitions have blinded us to opportunities.

We have bickered in factory and business, and sought to solve our differences only through self-interest.

Lord God of Hosts, forgive us! O God, by Thy guidance and Thy power may our beloved land once again become God's own country, a nation contrite in heart, confessing her sins; a nation keenly sensitive to all the unresolved injustice and wrong still in our midst.

Hear this our prayer and grant that we may confidently expect to see it answered in our time, through Jesus Christ, our Lord, Amen.[2]

Such balance is hard to find amid the polarized nature of current political discourse. May God restore the balance of this patriotism in both the church and the nation!

---

2. *The Prayers of Peter Marshall*, 95–96.

Appendix B

THE DIFFERENCES between the three approaches may be depicted diagrammatically:

Party-political Approach (*partisan*)	Biblical-political Approach (ethical/biblical worldview)	Apolitical Approach (*pietistic*)
Takes frequent breaks away from consecutive exposition in order to "preach" on historic-socio-political themes.	Maintains a regular diet of consecutive exposition.	Maintains a regular diet of "Gospel texts," or an apractical focus on Christ (redemptive-historical preaching).
More topical sermons (e.g., Christian roots of America, how evolution came to be taught in schools).	Expository sermons that reference burning contemporary issues as and when demanded by the text or passage of Scripture in view.	Curtails application of the preaching to the gospel (narrowly understood), issues of sanctification, and evangelism.
Typically assumes a party-political perspective—more often than not Republican in Euro-American congregations and Democratic in Afro-American or Hispanic congregations.	Allows the Word to speak for itself, both in terms of the range of issues addressed and the manner in which they are touched on. Sometimes the Word favors one party perspective, sometimes another; perhaps both parties; sometimes neither.	Typically makes application of the Word to but a narrow range of spiritual issues.
Often inspires partisan or party-political action.	Ought to inspire to a range of ecclesial, evangelistic, and socio-political activities, the motivation behind which is the biblical worldview.	Tends to be silent about political action, party-political or otherwise.

Appendix C

A Prayer for Our Politicians and Armed Forces[1]

ETERNAL GOD,
We come reverently before you today, conscious that we are small in your sight and have fallen short of your glory. Yet, in your mercy and your compassion, you call us to draw near to you. We do so humbly and gladly, in thankfulness for stable government and for the peace and prosperity we have generally enjoyed.

We beseech you that your blessing may rest upon these public servants. We thank you for them. Help them to govern aright. Grant them the insight of your Spirit into the issues with which they wrestle. Burden their hearts increasingly with the desire for honest investigation and presentation of fact. Help them to manage well loyalty to party with faithfulness to the common good. Resolve for them, we pray, conundrums that test to the limits, and beyond, the abilities of their human minds, and enable them to bring forth laws that concur with your will and are pleasing in your sight. Grant them protection, O God, from the temptations of power, and cause them to grow in satisfaction as they work for the enhancement of this Commonwealth. Impress upon them not only their accountability to the electorate, but ultimately their accountability to you. Protect, we beseech you, the unity of their marriages, and the welfare of their children; and grant them the benefit of a responsible media.

---

1. Tim J. R. Trumper, opening prayer as Guest Chaplain, Pennsylvania State Senate, Harrisburg, Wednesday January 24, 2007.

Finally, we call upon you for those of our armed forces from this Commonwealth serving you today in great danger. Watch over them we pray, grant their service success. Work good in their hearts through the trauma of their experiences, and return them in safety to their loved ones. For those families that grieve we ask your great grace.

All these things *I* ask in the name of Jesus, through his merits, and by the enabling of the Holy Spirit. Amen.

Bibliography

"Archbishop Attacks Public Atheism." No pages. Accessed on November 11, 2006. Online: http://news.bbc.co.uk/2/hi/uk_news/6138486.stm.

Barth, Karl. *Homiletics*. Translated by Geoffrey W. Bromiley and Donald E. Daniels. Louisville, KY: Westminster/John Knox Press, 1991.

Bishopthorpe, Lord Blanch of. "Is There any Word from the Lord?" In *Christianity & Conservatism: Are Christianity and Conservatism Compatible?* Edited by The Rt Hon. Michael Alison MP and David L. Edwards, 80–98. London et al.: Hodder & Stoughton, 1990.

Boateng, Paul. "The Hope of Things to Come." In *Reclaiming the Ground: Christianity & Socialism*, edited by Christopher Bryant, 53–66. London: Spire (Hodder and Stoughton), 1993.

Boice, James Montgomery. "The Preacher and Scholarship." In *The Preacher and Preaching: Reviving the Art in the Twentieth Century*, edited by Samuel T. Logan Jr., 91–104. Phillipsburg, NJ: Presbyterian and Reformed, 1986.

Bonhoeffer, Dietrich. *Letters & Papers from Prison*. London and Glasgow: Collins (Fontana Books), 1959.

Bopp, James. "Do's and Don'ts for Political Activities for Pastors." James Madison Center for Free Speech in association with the Alliance Defense Fund, March 2006.

Brookhiser, Richard. *What Would the Founders Do? Our Questions, Their Answers*. New York: Basic Books, 2006.

Bryant, Christopher. *Reclaiming the Ground: Christianity & Socialism*. London: Spire (Hodder and Stoughton), 1993.

Buchanan, Pat. *State of Emergency: The Third World Invasion and Conquest of America*. New York: St. Martin's Press, 2006.

Budziszewski, J. *Evangelicals in the Public Square: Four Formative Voices on Political Thought and Action*. Grand Rapids, MI: Baker Academic, 2006.

Campolo, Tony. *Is Jesus a Republican or a Democrat? And 14 other Polarizing Issues*. Dallas et al.: Word Publishing, 1995.

Churchill, Winston. *The Great Republic: A History of America*, edited by Winston S. Churchill. New York: Random House, 2000.

Colson, Charles with Ellen Santilli Vaughn, *God & Government: An Insider's View on the Boundaries between Faith & Politics*. Grand Rapids, MI: Zondervan, 2007.

Coulter, Ann. *How to Speak to a Liberal (If You Must): The World According to Ann Coulter*. New York, NY: Crown Forum, 2004.

D'Souza, Dinesh. *What's So Great About Christianity?* Washington, DC: Regnery Publishing Inc., 2007.

Demarest, Bruce A. "Revelation, General." In *Evangelical Dictionary of Theology*, edited by Walter A. Elwell, 944–45. Carlisle, U.K., and Grand Rapids, MI: Paternoster Press and Baker Books, 1984.

Ferguson, Sinclair B. "Exegesis." In *The Preacher and Preaching: Reviving the Art in the Twentieth Century*, edited by Samuel T. Logan Jr., 192–211. Phillipsburg, NJ: Presbyterian and Reformed, 1986.

Gorenstein, Nathan. "Shootings Ravage City Neighborhoods." *The Philadelphia Inquirer*, Sunday March 20, 2005. Accessed January 28, 2009. Online: http://www.philly.com/mld/inquirer/11180561.htm.

Hiebert, Paul G. *Transforming Worldviews: An Anthropological Understanding of How People Change*. Grand Rapids, MI: Baker Academic, 2008.

Hughes, John. Forthcoming *Festschrift* for John Frame. Philipsburg, NJ: P&R, 2009.

Hynes, Patrick. *In Defense of the Religious Right: Why Conservative Christians Are the Lifeblood of the Republican Party and Why that Terrifies the Democrats*. Nelson Current, 2006.

"In the World of Good and Evil." *The Economist* (September 14, 2006), 37. Accessed January 28, 2009. Online: No page. http://www.economist.com/world/unitedstates/displaystory.cfm?story_id=7912626.

Kennedy, D. James. *Will the Church Forget?* Fort Lauderdale, FL: Coral Ridge Ministries, 1997.

Kinnaman, David and Gabe Lyon. *unChristian: What a New Generation Really Thinks about Christianity . . . and Why It Matters*. Grand Rapids, MI: Baker Books, 2007.

———. "unChristian: What a New Generation Really Thinks about Christianity . . . and Why It Matters." The January Series. Calvin College, Grand Rapids, MI, January 22, 2009.

Kuo, J. David. "Putting Faith Before Politics." In *The New York Times*, November 16, 2006.

———. *Tempting Faith: An Inside Story of Political Seduction*. New York, et al.: Free Press, 2006.

Kuyper, Abraham. *Lectures on Calvinism*, reprint ed. Grand Rapids, MI: William B. Eerdmans, 1994.

Lewis, C. S. *Fern-seed and Elephants and other Essays on Christianity*, edited by Walter Hooper. Reprint ed. Glasgow: Collins (Fount Paperbacks), 1977.

Lewis, Ted. *Electing Not to Vote: Christian Reflections on Reasons for Not Voting*. Eugene, OR: Wipf and Stock, 2008.

Lloyd-Jones, D. M. "The Weapons of Our Warfare." In *Knowing the Times: Addresses Delivered on Various Occasions 1942–1977*. Edinburgh: The Banner of Truth Trust, 1989.

MacDonald, Gordon. "Leader's Insight: When Leaders Implode." *LeadershipJournal.net*. Pages 1–5. Accessed January 28, 2009. Online: http://www.christianitytoday.com/le/currenttrendscolumns/leadershipweekly/cln61106.html.

Macleod, Donald. "Preaching and Systematic Theology." In *The Preacher and Preaching: Reviving the Art in the Twentieth Century*, edited by Samuel T. Logan Jr., 246–72. Phillipsburg, NJ: Presbyterian and Reformed, 1986.

Maritain, Jacques. *The Twilight of Civilization*. Translated by Lionel Landry. London: Sheed and Ward, 1946.

Marshall, Catherine, *A Man Called Peter: The Story of Peter Marshall*, new paperback ed. Grand Rapids, MI: Chosen Books, 2002.

———. *The Prayers of Peter Marshall*. New York et al.: McGraw-Hill Book Company, 1954.

Maxwell, John C. *Ethics 101: What Every Leader Needs to Know*. New York et al.: Center Street, 2003.

Niemöller, Martin. *Dachau Sermons*. Translated by Robert H. Pfeiffer. New York and London: Harper & Brothers, 1946.

Noll, Mark A. *Adding Cross to Crown: The Political Significance of Christ's Passion*. Washington, DC and Grand Rapids, MI: The Center for Public Justice and Baker Book House, 1996.

Packer, J. I. "Introduction: Why Preach?" In *The Preacher and Preaching: Reviving the Art in the Twentieth Century*, edited by Samuel T. Logan Jr., 1–29. Phillipsburg, NJ: Presbyterian and Reformed, 1986.

Paisley, Rhonda. *Ian Paisley: My Father*. Basingstoke, Hants: Marshall Morgan and Scott, 1988.

Paxman, Jeremy. *The English: A Portrait of a People*, first published 1998. London: Penguin, 1999.

Pennings, Ray. "Political Ministers of God." In Joel R. Beeke et al., *Living for God's Glory: An Introduction to Calvinism*, 361–73. Orlando, FL: Reformation Trust Publishing (Ligonier Ministries), 2008.

Ramm, Bernard L. *Hermeneutics*. Grand Rapids, MI: Baker Book House, 1971.

"Reflections of a Lifetime Theologian: An Extended Interview with John M. Frame." *Christian Culture*, 1: 1–8 (April 2008).

Ryle, J. C. *Expository Thoughts on Luke*. Carlisle, Pennsylvania, and Edinburgh: The Banner of Truth Trust, 1986.

Savage, Michael. *The Political Zoo*. Nashville, TN: Nelson Current, 2006.

Schaeffer, Francis. *A Christian Manifesto*. In *The Complete Works of Francis Schaeffer: A Christian Worldview*, vol. 5; 2nd ed. Westchester, IL: Crossway, 1982.

Skillen, James W. "Where Kingdom Politics Should Lead Us." In Mark A. Noll, *Adding Cross to Crown: The Political Significance of Christ's Passion*, 79–90. Washington, DC and Grand Rapids, MI: The Center for Public Justice and Baker Book House, 1996.

Stafford, Tim. "Evangelism Plus: John Stott reflects on where we've been and where we're going." *Christianity Today* 50:10 (October 2006), 99. Accessed January 28, 2009. Online: http://www.ctlibrary.com/ct/2006/october/32.94html.

Stott, John R. W. *I Believe in Preaching* (U.S. title: *Between Two Worlds*). London et al.: Hodder and Stoughton, 1982.

———. *The Message of the Sermon on the Mount: Christian Counter-Culture*. The Bible Speaks Today. Reprint ed. Leicester, England, and Downers Grove, IL: IVP, 1990.

Thatcher, Margaret. "A Speech by the Prime Minister, 21 May 1988." In *Christianity & Conservatism: Are Christianity and Conservatism Compatible?* Edited by The Rt Hon. Michael Alison MP and David L. Edwards, 333–38. London et al.: Hodder & Stoughton, 1990.

Thomas, Cal and Bob Beckel. *Common Ground: How to Stop the Partisan War That Is Destroying America.* New York, NY: William Morrow (Harper Collins), 2007.

Thomas, Cal and Ed Dobson. *Blinded by Might: Why the Religious Right Can't Save America.* Grand Rapids, MI: Zondervan, 1999.

Trumper, Tim J. R. "Prayer for the President Elect." Sermon preached from 1 Timothy 2:1–2 on November 9, 2008, at Seventh Reformed Church, Grand Rapids, MI (www.7thref.org).

Wallis, Jim. *God's Politics: How the Right Gets It Wrong and the Left Doesn't Get It.* New York, NY: Harper One (Harper Collins), 2005.

Wilson, A. N. *God's Funeral.* London: Abacus, 1999.

Also published by Wipf and Stock:

Tim J. R. Trumper, *When History Teaches Us Nothing: The Recent Reformed Sonship Debate in Context.*

Tim J. R. Trumper (Ph.D., University of Edinburgh) is Senior Minister of Seventh Reformed Church, Grand Rapids, Michigan (www.7thref.org). Previously he taught systematic theology at Westminster Theological Seminary, Philadelphia, and has pastored in South-East Pennsylvania.

www.ingramcontent.com/pod-product-compliance
Lightning Source LLC
Chambersburg PA
CBHW070929160426
43193CB00011B/1622